ENCOUNTER

SERIES

1. *Virtue—Public and Private*

2. *Unsecular America*

3. *Confession, Conflict, and Community*

4. *Democracy and the Renewal of Public Education*

5. *The Bible, Politics, and Democracy*

6. *Jews in Unsecular America*

7. *The Believable Futures of American Protestantism*

8. *The Preferential Option for the Poor*

9. *Biblical Interpretation in Crisis: The Ratzinger Conference on Bible and Church*

10. *American Apostasy: The Triumph of "Other" Gospels*

11. *Law and the Ordering of Our Life Together*

12. *Reinhold Niebuhr Today*

13. *Guaranteeing the Good Life: Medicine and the Return of Eugenics*

14. *The Structure of Freedom: Correlations, Causes, and Cautions*

The Structure of Freedom: Correlations, Causes, and Cautions

Essays by

Peter L. Berger
Raymond Duncan Gastil
George Weigel

and
The Story of an Encounter by

Paul T. Stallsworth

Edited and with a Foreword by

Richard John Neuhaus

WILLIAM B. EERDMANS PUBLISHING COMPANY
GRAND RAPIDS, MICHIGAN

Published by Wm. B. Eerdmans Publishing Co.
in cooperation with
The Rockford Institute Center on Religion & Society

Library of Congress Cataloging-in-Publication Data

Berger, Peter L.
    The structure of freedom: correlations, causes, and cautions / essays
by Peter L. Berger, Raymond Duncan Gastil, George Weigel; and The
story of an encounter by Paul T. Stallsworth; edited and with a
foreword by Richard John Neuhaus.
    p.   cm.
  ISBN 0-8028-0214-1
  1. Liberty. I. Gastil, Raymond D. II. Weigel, George. III. Neuhaus,
Richard John. IV. Stallsworth, Paul T. The story of an encounter.
V. Title.
JC585.B397   1991
323'.01—dc20   90-21445
                                      CIP

Contents

Foreword   vii

Peter L. Berger
   The Serendipity of Liberties   1

Raymond Duncan Gastil
   Conflicting Freedoms:
   Individual and Collective   18

George Weigel
   Religious Freedom:
   The First Human Right   34

Paul T. Stallsworth
   The Story of an Encounter   56

Participants   141

Foreword

You can tell from the subtitle of this book—"Correlations, Causes, and Cautions"—that this is a discussion of many parts. But are the many parts of freedom really all of a piece? Religious freedom, political freedom, economic freedom—do they all stand or fall together?

Some of the participants in this discussion emphasize correlations, the things that seem to happen together. Others go farther and suggest that "correlations" is too weak a term; what we're really talking about are causal connections. And, especially in the last part of the discussion, all agree on the need for cautions in order to discipline our culture's frequently loose talk about freedom itself.

You are invited to join in the discussion. Indeed, I expect it will be hard not to join in the back and forth, the thrust and counterthrust, of the "Story of an Encounter." This is a diverse and spirited group of participants. At one point the claim is made that the group is predominantly conservative or neoconservative, but that claim does not go unchallenged. In fact, it becomes clear that this is in critical ways a very liberal conversation. Some participants heap disdain on that term of opprobrium, "liberal individualism." And yet it is generally acknowledged that we are carrying on this conversation within a context strongly marked by liberal individualism. Not only is that acknowledged, but it is in important ways appreciatively affirmed, at least by most of the conferees. After all, some of the freedoms we care most about are closely tied to liberal individualism. Certainly that is true historically, but not only is it a truth about the past. At present we want to maintain the gains for freedom that came out of a liberal individualistic tradition, but we also want to ground those gains more securely in truths about community and the common good.

The three spheres of freedom under discussion—religious, political, and economic—elicit quite different responses. This is evident in the opening discussion about connections between political and economic freedoms. Economic freedom usually goes by the name of capitalism—a name that arouses strong emotions in contemporary debates. One question addressed is whether the term "democratic capitalism" represents merely a historical correlation, such as we experience in the United States, or a connection stronger than that. As you might expect, there is lively dispute about Peter Berger's claim that economic freedom is a necessary, but not sufficient, cause of political freedom. That claim does not sit well with those who prefer something like "democratic socialism" and who insist that, historical setbacks to the contrary, the term is not oxymoronic.

In numerous discussions today, also in the churches, it is argued that we should strive for a "third way"—something quite different from either capitalism or socialism. Some of the participants in this discussion insist that the search for a "third way" is illusory and self-defeating. All the conceivable or practicable alternatives, it is said, are contained in varying mixes of what we know as capitalism and socialism. Although it came out after our discussion, Pope John Paul II's encyclical entitled *Sollicitudo Rei Socialis* is pertinent to this question. There the pope emphatically stated that the church does not represent a "third way" between capitalism and socialism. And yet, were justice served, the result might not look very much like what we know as capitalism or socialism today. This dispute over the "third way" is of utmost urgency in our time. If, as Berger and others argue, it is illusory, talk about the "third way" is simply getting in the way of our making the necessary decisions about the course of freedom in the contemporary world.

There is a powerful element of what might be called prescience in this exchange. Please remember that this conference was held prior to the "Revolution of 1989" in Central and Eastern Europe. By the end of 1990, it was apparent to all but the purblind that talk about a "third way," "socialism with a human face," and "social market economy" was empty chatter. For a while, some Communist parties changed their name to Socialist, but the driving forces in these newly liberated societies were set upon a clean break with their disastrous past. Not everybody was as blunt as the leading economist of Solidarity in Poland. "Our purpose," he declared, "is to move as fast as possible away from Communism, through the remnants of socialism, toward Reaganism." And, of course, the most important changes, as Vaclav Havel of Czechoslovakia and others underscored, were not economic but cultural. The Revolution of 1989 was a historic break toward the reconstitution of "civil society." This means the mix of habits and institutions—including the economic, to be sure—that make possible what this book calls the "structure of freedom." What happened in Eastern Europe—and what, God willing, continues to happen in the years ahead—is a momentous working out in social reality of the arguments joined in the present discussion.

All in all, this is an unusually provocative discussion, and I would not attempt to summarize even the chief points engaged. I should say that I was most particularly struck by the dialogue on law and its connection with the freedoms examined here. That dialogue is woven throughout the encounter, but it is given sharpest expression by Mary Ann Glendon of the Harvard Law School. Do we have, she asks, an unqualified commitment to "law as command" which is grounded exclusively in individual rights? Do we just "make" law in order to accommodate entitlements? Or is law also a reflection of lived experience in community, even of some shared vision of the common good? These questions are deeply disturbing but also promising. They drive to the heart of current debates about abortion, distributive justice, welfare policy, and much else.

At one point Andrew Sullivan, formerly of *The New Republic,* perhaps being somewhat naughty, urges that our only shared idea of the common good is the good of relativism. In reply he gets the forceful response that he undoubtedly wanted to provoke. And that discussion, which takes place toward the end of the encounter, must be related back to George Weigel's argument that religious freedom is the source and safeguard of all freedoms. This is one important instance that illustrates how the conversation does not always proceed step by step in a linear fashion. Issues raised in one paper are answered in another, points established early in the discussion are thrown into question a little later in the discussion. This interweaving, this circling around, this thrust and counterthrust underscores in my mind the ways in which the freedoms addressed are all of a piece. That is not a triumphant conclusion. It is, I hope, an informed and nuanced discernment of the reality. The reader too, I expect, will not discover this to be a book of triumphant conclusions. I am confident, however, that those who read it will be rewarded by a clearer understanding of the correlations, causes, and cautions of the structure of freedom—religious, political, and economic.

The meeting from which this book emerges was co-sponsored by the Center on Religion & Society in New York City and the Institute for the Study of Economic Culture at Boston University. Peter Berger and I are especially grateful to Maria McFadden, Paul Stallsworth, and Davida Goldman, without whom—truth requires and friendship impels our saying—this book would not be.

NEW YORK CITY   Richard John Neuhaus

The Serendipity of Liberties

Peter L. Berger

The topic of this conference is the connection between political, economic, and religious liberties. There are, of course, many theories about this connection, and one thing that is at least mildly interesting is that there are theories on both the Right and the Left of the ideological spectrum that hold this connection to be intrinsic, inevitable, and inexorable. On the Right, as presently understood in the United States, there is frequently the notion that there is a necessary and inexorable nexus between political and economic liberties; this translates itself into the belief that the institutional systems of democracy and capitalism are necessarily and inexorably linked. Religious liberty figures here as one of the prime beneficiaries of this linkage. The Left is typically uninterested in religion, but theories on the Left also maintain a necessary connection between what *they* consider to be political and economic liberties. The common argument here is that political liberty, as institutionalized in democracy, is unreal, a sham, unless grounded in economic liberty, by which is understood the surpassing of alienation and want intended by socialism. So in the truly socialist society there is (or, more cautiously, will be in the future) an inexorable unity of political and economic liberty.

While my own position is more to the Right than to the Left, I must confess that neither set of theories strikes me as persuasive. The ideas of the Left fly in the face of all the evidence

1

that I know, a point that I will come to shortly. But the theories of the Right that propose this indissoluble unity of all liberties seem to me to assert axiomatically what remains to be demonstrated empirically. And what is troublesome about most of these theories is their abstract character and their overly rational view of human society. All too often what appears necessary in the mind turns out to be far from necessary in empirical reality, and conversely the most illogical, even absurd relations between ideas and institutions confront us as hard empirical facts in what is generally taken to be the real world. Whatever history is, it is *not* the march of reason on earth. Rather, it is a messy, disorderly, mostly irrational constellation of shifting interests and passions. Serendipity, not logical consistency, marks its course.

This does not imply, of course, that the mind will not try to impose order, or that the actor in history will not seek to realize some measure of order that makes sense to him. But both rational understanding and rational action must reckon with the facticity of the irrational and, most important, with the fact of unintended consequences. Distressing though this is, it is a fact that most of our actions do not lead to the consequences we intended or anticipated. I would contend, following Max Weber, that this fact is the single most important insight to be derived from the modern historical and social sciences. And that is why overly rational designs for human life, both individual and collective, have created so much havoc. In one of his essays Octavio Paz calls such designs "syllogism-daggers"—an apt and haunting phrase! Theories can kill, as we should have learned, and at least one reason for this is the result of all efforts to force the messy reality of human life onto a theoretical procrustean bed: if a limb here or there won't fit, it must be cut off. This is why careful attention to the empirical is not only an intellectual but also a moral good. And herein also lies the superiority of Adam Smith over Karl Marx—not in the details of economic analysis (which, I daresay, leaves much to be desired in either case), but in Smith's insight that human benefits come from an "invisible hand" (that is, from logically implausible but empirically discernible connections) as against the Marxian project of improving the human condition by imposing a relentlessly rational design.

Let us begin with political liberty, which in its most commonsensical sense means that individuals and groups are institutionally protected against arbitrary power through participation in the shaping of this power. This is the reality implied by the phrase "liberal democracy," a phrase which must be unpacked. The adjective commonly refers to respect for the rights and liberties of people. The noun "democracy," of course, has been used in recent times by every conceivable regime and, in international political discourse today, means precisely nothing. But, following a wide consensus in American political science, I would propose that the most useful employment of the term refers to very specific institutional arrangements, all designed to make government more accountable and more limited in its exercise of power. These arrangements include regular elections, rights of political expression and opposition, and the expectation that governments voted out of office will in fact leave and that the people voted in will in fact take over government power.

Now, if the phrase "liberal democracy" is unpacked in this way, it becomes quite clear that there is no necessary or inevitable connection between its adjective and its noun. Nondemocratic regimes can be liberal: suffice it to mention that some great liberal reforms were initiated in Europe in the era of Enlightened absolutism—in Austria, for example, judicial torture was abolished by Maria Theresa, capital punishment by her son Joseph II, who also granted religious liberty to Protestants and greatly ameliorated the civil status of Jews. And in our time there are old-fashioned despotic regimes that are fairly liberal when it comes to various areas on human life. (I'm thinking here of some of the governments on the Arabian peninsula.) Conversely, democratic regimes can be and have been very illiberal in some areas and sometimes across the board. Democracy, after all, institutionalizes the rule of majorities, and we have known since Aristotle that a majority can be tyrannical. In modern Western history Jacobinism represents paradigmatically this potential tyranny of the majority, of which Jean-Jacques Rousseau was the prophet and to which J. L. Talmon has given the ominous name "totalitarian democracy."

It is empirical serendipity, not philosophical logic, that nonetheless gives validity to the phrase "liberal democracy." The validity is statistical—a matter of frequency distribution, if you will—but I think that this enhances rather than diminishes its force. In empirical fact, there is indeed a very high correlation between democracy on the one hand and the protection of rights and liberties on the other. The statistical character of this linkage allows us to stipulate, without fear of cognitive dissonance, that, indeed, there are liberal despots and illiberal democracies. Let us rejoice in Arabian potentates who respect the privacy of the home or the free movement of their subjects. Let us, by all means, deplore illiberal actions of democratically elected governments in the United States or anywhere else. The fact remains that *most of the time* despots act illiberally and democracies protect liberties. I will certainly defer to Raymond Gastil in this matter, but I think he will agree (and the lovely little lists that Freedom House provides us with every year will, I think, bear me out) that the correlation between the two phenomena is striking. Make one map of the world that indicates the existence of democratic institutions— regular elections, opposition parties, freedom of political organization, and so on. Then make another map that registers the places where violations of basic human rights are rare or nonexistent. And then superimpose one map onto the other. The two maps will not coincide perfectly. Very little in human life coincides perfectly. But the two maps coincide sufficiently to allow the empirical proposition (like all such propositions, a statistical one) that democracy and respect for human rights tend to go together.

Now, to say that this linkage is serendipitous may be slightly misleading if it suggests that there are no reasons for the linkage; the serendipity must be asserted only against such theories that, a priori, maintain the linkage to be necessary and therefore universal. How, then, is one to explain the empirical linkage? This is not too difficult, it seems to me. The explanation must be in terms of the nature of the modern state and its historically unprecedented concentration of power, which is the result of modern technology and the controls it makes possible.

When I read about premodern regimes, I am always impressed by how limited their power was in comparison with that of even the most feeble and moderate government in modern times. We are certainly justified in viewing, say, the Roman Empire as a very great concentration of power. Yet, in the lives of most ordinary people, especially those who lived far away from Rome as putative subjects of Rome, the power of the empire was usually remote and only sporadically experienced (when, for instance, Rome sent out an army to quell a rebellion or impose its will on a recalcitrant subject people). For most of the people most of the time, the empire was an abstract entity that only occasionally intruded into their real lives. I would not be surprised if there were large numbers of people, supposedly within the borders of the empire, who had never heard of it. I don't want to generalize incautiously. There may have been exceptions to my proposition—the Inca Empire, with its near-totalitarian control over every detail of its subjects' lives, suggests itself as an exception. But even there one must wonder, as one looks at a map of the vast territory over which the Incas supposedly held sway, how real the central power was as one moved away from Cuzco into remote jungles and mountain valleys.

Be that as it may, today even the government of a fragile banana-republic-type state is equipped with communications and transport that allow it to penetrate, not sporadically but in a continuous fashion, every corner of its sovereign territory. What is more, even such a government has under its control a network of institutions—police stations, radio stations, schools, post offices, highway maintenance posts, airfields, and so on—which blanket its territory in a way that was, if not impossible, certainly very difficult to establish under premodern conditions. Here one does not even have to think of the modern means of repression. Take instead two fundamental manifestations of the modern state—mass education and mass taxation. Both have created historically unprecedented institutions of control—one over the minds, the other over the daily labor of its subjects.

Democracies are by no means exceptions to this general character of the modern state. Take the most democratic regime you can think of—Switzerland?—or, even better, one little Swiss canton?—and I would argue that the power to control and coerce at its disposal far exceeds that of the Caesars (or, for that matter, of Genghis Khan). But above all, democracy means one thing—the establishment of routine (that is, institutionalized) limits to the power of the state. It is instructive to peruse the by-now sizable literature of so-called democracy theory. But in the end, democracy boils down to two very simple projects: that we have a chance periodically to kick the bastards out, and that there are limits to what they can do to us while they are in! This limitation on the power of the state protects rights and liberties *not* because the electorate is wise and will always (or even usually) elect good rulers, but because human nature is such that power held without limits will almost inevitably lead to exercises in tyranny. Perhaps one should add that such constraint is especially important under modern conditions, and the reason for this is rather simple too. In addition to the aforementioned fact that rulers in pre-modern societies lacked the technological means of control they command today, it is also true that their power was limited by tradition—kinship, tribe, caste, priesthoods, and the like being the institutional forms through which tradition exercised its countervailing power. Modernization tends to undermine and weaken these traditional restraints on tyrannical excesses. The traditional despot, however bloody-minded, often had to worry about what tribal elders, shamans, or prophets could do to him, and he may also have been restrained, if not by morality, then at least by superstitious fears. Most modern tyrants are relatively free of these handicaps. To prevent the bastards in power from doing their worst, then, democracy is left as the best bet.

Let me suggest an imaginative experiment to you. One of the more interesting and appealing institutions in classical China was that of the imperial censors. These were officials schooled in Confucian learning who were attached to the court in Peking. Their mission was to point out and rebuke incorrect behavior on the part of the government, including even the emperor himself. Now, I'm enough of a sociologist (and, therefore, enough of a skeptic) to suspect that these gentlemen were not always zealous in the execution of their official duties; I suspect that some of them could be bought off or intimidated into prudent silence. Yet Chinese history records a number of instances in which imperial censors heroically denounced government atrocities, sometimes paying for this with their lives. And it is not hard to believe that even some very nasty emperors tried to avoid acts that might provoke the censors to denounce them—and perhaps even to question the mandate of heaven by which they claimed legitimacy. But let me come to the imaginative experiment. Try to impose on your mind a Rawlsian "veil of ignorance" about anything you now know about the modern world. Then ask yourself how, in a world that has no powerful and unchallenged tradition like that of Confucianism, one could design institutions that might constitute a functional equivalent to the imperial censors. My bet is that you will come up with something like the institutions of liberal democracy. In other words, given the structures of modernity, if liberal democracy did not exist, it would have to be invented. Luckily for us, it *was* invented, and in this invention lies our best empirical hope not to be afflicted by all the atrocities to which untrammeled power is prone.

What I have here called empirical serendipity deepens as we move from political to economic liberties. Once again, of course, there are theories embodying very different notions about what "economic liberties" might mean. It is the Right that is more prone to use the phrase, and often what it means by the phrase is the exercise of "property rights." I have no great trouble with this concept, unless it is embedded in some a priori theory about the ontological grounding of these rights. The Left prefers to speak of "economic rights," which refer to such matters as the putative right to employment or safe working conditions or health insurance. My difficulty with this (which has often been the difficulty of the United States in international discussions of human rights) is only that it is counterproductive to include every possible good under the rubric of "rights." Be that as it may, it is fairly clear, I think, what most ordinary people in the world mean when they use phrases like "economic liberties" *or* "economic rights"—to be ensured the basic material necessities of life, to be able to enjoy the fruits of their work and to pass these on to their children, to be able as far as conditions permit to choose what work to do and how and where to work, and (last, not least) to be allowed to try to improve their condition. I don't claim, of course, that this is a complete or universal list of economic desiderata, but I think it comes close to what most people expect, minimally, from an economy they will accept as just. It also means that keeping such ordinary desires in mind offers the best entrance to the discussion of the next linkage we must consider, the linkage that is usually intended when people on the Right speak of the relation between political and economic liberties—namely, the linkage between democracy and capitalism.

The word "capitalism" has not been as much devalued as the word "democracy," but here too there are many definitions, some of them intentionally pejorative rather than descriptive. This is not the place to go into this matter in any detail (and, having published a book on this subject entitled *The Capitalist Revolution*, I can make things easier for myself by simply referring to it). Suffice it to say here that most definitions of capitalism (including Marxist ones) contain three basic elements: capitalism is, to use Marx's phrase, a *"mode of production"* (which has the important implication that capitalism as well as socialism, its major alternative, should not be primarily understood in terms of distribution); capitalism means production determined by *market forces* (and not by a system of political decisions); and under capitalism the basic means of production are *privately owned*. It is further assumed by such description (as it was emphatically assumed by Marx) that capitalism as an economic system develops a dynamism of great power which operates autonomously vis-à-vis other institutions of society (as compared, for example, with a feudal system, which is relatively static economically and in which the economy is embedded in other, non-economic structures). Again, without necessarily accepting the details Adam Smith implied by the "invisible hand," I think the phrase indicates an important feature of capitalism: once established, it appears to "run" on its own, following its own inherent logic, like an engine that has been turned on; very often it is difficult for the people who are supposed to be in charge of it to control it or even understand it.

One of the recurrent errors in contemporary social thought (on the Right as much as on the Left) is to confuse the consequences of modernization with the consequences of a particular mode of production. Modernization is the global process of transformation brought about by technology, and it has certain consequences regardless of the manner in which economic life is organized. Under modern conditions, there are really only two such forms of organization—those broadly labeled "capitalism" (as previously defined) and "socialism" (defined, conversely, as production based on political decisions rather than on the market and with public ownership of the means of production). It is important *not* to ascribe to either capitalism or socialism effects that *both* experience under the impact of modernization—such as all of the discontents (or, if you will, "alienations") of a pluralized and urbanized society, or the difficulties of governance in an increasingly complex society, or the redundance of large segments of the labor force due to technological changes.

As I have argued in *The Capitalist Revolution* (I cannot repeat the argument here), one of the most significant of these *common* consequences of modernization is the pattern of income distribution. The forces that appear to drive income distribution (expressed over time in the so-called Kuznets Curve) are grounded in demography and the labor demands of a technologized economy, and the resulting pattern of income distribution is remarkably similar when one compares societies of whatever mode of production at similar stages of economic growth. This implies that much of the contemporary debate on "inequality" is empirically irrelevant, at least if it is assumed to have some bearing on the issue of capitalism versus socialism. One may add (since, as perhaps I should have pointed out before, capitalism and socialism manifest themselves empirically not as absolute alternatives but in gradations on a continuum of possibilities) that the "tyranny of the Kuznets Curve," as some have called it, is just as much evident in cases of "mixed economies." Put simply, whatever measure of inequality one finds in a modern society, one should assign "blame" (or, for that matter, credit) *not* to that society's mode of production but rather to its degree of modernization. There is certainly no empirical basis for the belief that socialism leads to a higher degree of equality.

What capitalism demonstrably does result in, as compared with socialism, is a cornucopia of material benefits spilled out over an increasing (and in recent times a dramatically increasing) proportion of the population. What has happened in advanced capitalist societies is the precise opposite of Marx's prophecy of "immiseration": the proletariat has *not* become poorer as the capitalist class became richer; on the contrary, misery of the sort described by, say, Charles Dickens in the early days after the Industrial Revolution has virtually disappeared from these societies, and their working classes now enjoy a standard of living that would have aroused the envy of the aristocracies of the *ancien régime*. What is more, the later Marxist attempt to cope with the falsification of the immiseration theory by arguing that, yes, the advanced capitalist societies have gained, but only at the expense of the impoverished societies of the Third World, has also been in process of falsification because a number of these societies have "made it"—not despite capitalism, but because of it, and regardless of their state of "dependency." The most important falsification of these neo-Marxist theories derives from the capitalist societies of East Asia, beginning with Japan, including the so-called Four Little Dragons (South Korea, Taiwan, Hong Kong, and Singapore), with this crescent of prosperity now advancing into most of the capitalist societies of Southeast Asia.

If, then, one wants to speak the language of "economic rights"—or, in the phrase coined by the liberation theologians, of the "preferential option for the poor"—one must say, on empirical grounds, that capitalism provides the best guarantees for "economic rights" and the best chance of moving large masses of the poor from degrading misery up to a decent standard of living. One may argue about the role of the state in making this process less painful, more rapid, or more equitable—this is the major political argument between sane people on the Right and the Left in Western democracies. In other words, there is room for argument about the redistributive role of government. If one sticks to the empirical evidence, however, there is really no argument anymore about which mode of production will best generate the wealth that may be redistributed: it is capitalism. But what about the relationship of this economic bonanza to political liberties?

It is clearly possible to have capitalism without democracy. It started out that way in Europe (seen from below, England at the time of the Industrial Revolution was a brutally repressive oligarchy), as it did in Japan, and many of the most successful "new industrial societies" in Asia are ruled by authoritarian regimes. One can modify this picture by stating that some democracies have also embarked on successful capitalist development (for example, Malaysia and Sri Lanka), so that there is no reason to embrace the pessimistic thesis that dictatorship is *necessary* for a successful capitalist "takeoff." One may also point out that, when capitalist development has been sufficiently successful to produce a large, reasonably affluent middle class, pressures *toward* democracy are commonly generated (see, for instance, current events in South Korea and Taiwan). Still, much though I would like to do so, I cannot conscientiously say that you cannot have capitalism without democracy. I'm happy to report, however, that the converse proposition can be made on much firmer empirical grounds: it appears that you cannot have democracy without capitalism.

The evidence on this is clear and massive. As one looks at the contemporary world (if one liked, one could again superimpose maps here), one sees that there are indeed capitalist societies which are not democracies (though it is worth noting that, by now, none are in the advanced industrial societies). But all existing democracies have capitalist economies—indeed, are linked to the international capitalist system. And there is not a single socialist economy with a democratic regime. One may like or dislike these empirical correlations, depending on one's philosophical dispositions, but it seems to me that one will have to reckon with them if one is to look at the world honestly. These correlations have led me, for one, to a simple but far-reaching proposition: *Capitalism is the necessary but not sufficient condition of democracy.*

Once again, this relationship is more than serendipitous; there are reasons for it. And, once again, the principal reason has to do with the nature of the modern state. As I argued

previously, the modern state constitutes an enormous, historically unique concentration of power. This is true no matter
whether the economy in question is capitalist or socialist. But
what does the difference in the mode of production imply for
state power? Whatever socialism may mean in theory and in
the utopian imagination (where one may dream of free communities, spontaneous cooperation, the state withering away,
and such), in empirical reality, socialism means that *the state
runs the economy*—and this, mind you, *in addition to* the vast
power that the state already has. "Real existent socialism" (as
Marxists call it, as distinct from the salvific socialism of the
future) represents a quantum leap in state power. Put differently, when the state, in addition to all the other things it can
do to control people, also controls all sources or all significant
sources of employment, its power becomes near-absolute; then
there are, literally, no more avenues of escape. By contrast, in
capitalist societies with authoritarian regimes, *at least* the
economy escapes the direct control of the state; in such societies
one sees again and again how individuals with oppositionist
views find refuge in the private sector; in a socialist society
there is no private sector. Given these facts, it is hardly surprising that socialism is very unlikely to generate institutionalized
limits on the power of the state. Conversely, one can understand why capitalism, though it may not in itself tend toward
any particular form of government, provides the necessary
presupposition for democracy.

Socialism has a built-in authoritarian, probably a built-in
totalitarian tendency. Leaving aside the complex issue of totalitarianism (which, for understandable reasons, usually enrages
theorists of the Left), the classical doctrine of socialism understood this very well. That is why Marx insisted on the "dictatorship of the proletariat." Since, regrettably, the proletariat fails
to exist or has failed to exhibit the characteristics assigned to it
by Marxist theory, Lenin invented the Party as the "vanguard
of the proletariat," which very kindly exercises dictatorship on
behalf of the proletariat. But dictatorship it must be. Nor was
Marx wrong in his reasons for thinking this. Socialism is based
on an enormous act of expropriation, which can be accomplished only by coercion. But (and this Marx probably did *not*

understand) the expropriation cannot be a once-and-for-all event. Given human nature and the inner logic of economic activity, market forces and private ownership keep returning. Ergo, this "creeping capitalism" must be beaten down—again and again. The idea that, eventually, this coercive machinery will be disassembled—that the bourgeoisie will be dead for good, even the "remnants of bourgeois consciousness" will have disappeared, and the dictatorship will spontaneously dissolve in the historic "leap into freedom"—is a fantasy. It happens to be the regnant political fantasy of the twentieth century, an immensely powerful myth (in the sense of Georges Sorel). *That* is also an empirical fact, but it does not derive from the empirical facts about the economics and politics of modernity. Rather, it springs from those depths of the mind in which reside our dreams of redemption. This particular dream has possibly created more suffering and pain than any other dream in history, and the redemption it has aspired to has been a most terrible delusion.

Capitalism, on the other hand, has been singularly devoid of mythogenic capacity. It is a sober, practical, "uninspiring" thing. Historically (with few exceptions, I should think), it has derived its legitimations from elsewhere—from religion, or family loyalties, or nationalism. Yet, at least in America, there has been a widespread understanding (often implicit and inarticulate) that capitalism and democracy "go together." This popular understanding—"It's a free country!"—is not the illusion that many intellectuals have made it out to be. It is quite solidly based in empirical reality, certainly in the empirical reality of American history. The phrase "democratic capitalism," lately used with good effect by Michael Novak, is indeed an empirically available "package." Capitalism is not intrinsically or inexorably linked with democracy. But the linkage is there empirically, and for analyzable and comprehensible reasons. And, very important, capitalism *via* democracy is linked to the protection of human rights and liberties. Put simply, a "free country," in which arbitrary state power is restrained and in which human rights are respected, will with overwhelming likelihood be a capitalist country. When all the complexities have been dealt with, the pragmatic implication is breathtakingly simple: if you want democracy, you will have to take capitalism. Is this a sure thing? Of course not. There are very few sure things in the real world. But the bet on capitalism is a far, far surer thing than the homicidal gambles that have sprung from the socialist dream.

Is there need here for a separate discussion of religious liberty? Or does this constitute an unnecessary addition to the argument? On one level, of course, everything that has been said up to now about the relation of democracy, capitalism, and liberties applies to religious liberty. The latter, of course, is one of the human rights and liberties of which democracy is the best guarantor; and, insofar as democracy depends on capitalism, there is also an important connection between the latter and religious liberty. But there is another level on which religious liberty occupies a unique or near-unique place.

While religious liberty is *one* of the rights and liberties that must be given institutionalized protection from the grasp of state power, it can be argued that it is the single most important right and liberty. Let me emphasize that this is *not* a theological argument, though obviously such an argument might be made (not here, but elsewhere); in the Judeo-Christian context, such an argument would presumably start with the First Commandment. But in the present context a quite different argument can be made, a purely secular one (that is, I could make it even if, instead of being a Lutheran, I were an agnostic and possibly even if I were an atheist): *religious liberty is fundamental because it posits the ultimate limit on the power of the state.* Because of this, the status of religious liberty in a society is a very good *empirical* measure of the general condition of rights and liberties in that society.

Why should this be so? The reason lies at the very core of what religion is all about: religion intends transcendence. That is, it points beyond this world to realities utterly beyond (as Rudolf Otto put it, *totaliter aliter*) the reality of ordinary, everyday life. Needless to say, different religious traditions do this in vastly different ways, but transcendent intentionality is common to all of them. Indeed, transcendent intentionality is the foundational, the defining characteristic of that realm of human experience and thought which the term "religion" refers to. In pointing to the wholly other, religion ipso facto relativizes, puts in their proper place, all the realities of this world, including all institutions. This proper place, of course, is an inferior place—mundane, profane, penultimate. Religion, in other words, refuses to take with ultimate seriousness the solemn dramas of the social world: in biblical wording, God laughs at them—and the believer, by God's grace, is enabled to share in this laughter, even while he is still in this world, in anticipation of the final redemption which (I would argue this with great theological seriousness) will include cosmically comic relief.

This, alas, is not the right occasion to develop a theology of the comic. Let me only point out, quite nontheologically/sociologically, that no institution takes itself as seriously as the polity. Power is serious, self-consciously serious business. Religion put limits on this seriousness by viewing power *sub species aeternitatis*—a view that inevitably reduces, debunks, and thereby humanizes power. That, incidentally, accounts for the phenomenological resemblance between two prototypically subversive figures—the prophet and the clown. Put differently, religion limits the power of the state because it refuses to recognize the state's sovereignty as ultimate; religion posits *another* sovereignty beyond and indeed over that of the state.

It is for this reason that religious liberty is more than one item in a catalog of human rights. To be sure, as in the First Amendment, the right to the free exercise of religion can be juridically linked with other rights, such as the right to free assembly and free speech. There is nothing wrong with this linkage. But the state that guarantees religious liberty does more than acknowledge yet another human right: it acknowledges, perhaps without knowing it, that its power is less than ultimate. It seems to me, however, that throughout history many rulers have known that this is so. This explains why tyrants in general and modern totalitarian tyrannies in particular have been particularly eager to curtail religious liberty and to obtain control over religious institutions. Religion is the most powerful reminder of human finitude; tyrants tend to be individuals whose hubris is infinite and therefore individuals who find reminders of their own finitude intolerably offensive. Conversely, democracy, whose very essence is the limitation of state power, is always in need of firm guarantees of all the other rights and liberties, and indeed of the very legitimacy of the democratic state.

These considerations lead to an intriguing paradox. What I have just described can appropriately be called a secular service rendered by religion, a service to the world, if you will; yet *this worldly contribution of religion is possible only if religion itself remains otherworldly.* In recent years we have been told over and over again how religion must become more worldly, more of service to society, more "relevant" in terms of this or that social or political agenda. Leave aside here the fact that most of these agendas have been foolish or worse, as well as the fact that, of all institutions, religious ones are possibly the least qualified to render these services. Much more fundamental is the (admittedly paradoxical) fact that the worldly uses of religion will diminish to precisely the degree that religious institutions themselves become more worldly. I suppose that, even apart from the preceding considerations, this should not surprise us too much: any institution remains "relevant" as long as it has something distinctive to offer. Religious institutions are no exception. The religious institution that becomes indistinguishable from other institutions, such as political lobbies or therapeutic agencies or radical caucuses (or, needless to add, conservative caucuses), in very short order has great difficulty answering the question of why it should exist as a separate institution at all. At this point it has become "irrelevant" in the strictest sense of the word—the sense of redundancy and obsolescence. (Under the circumstances, let me add, this is a well-deserved fate.)

I must come to a conclusion. I have used the word "serendipity" in the title of this essay. I intended thereby to convey the unexpected (though, as I have tried to show, not accidental) empirical connection between several complexes of human society. Serendipity occurs when one sets out to sail for India and discovers America, when one goes to a business meeting and falls in love, perhaps when one starts out doing sociology and ends up with philosophy. Both democracy and capitalism, as social constructions, have a prosaic, sober, matter-of-fact quality. They are practical institutional arrangements made to achieve fairly limited purposes—to prevent the arbitrary exercise of power and to facilitate the production of wealth. How impoverished a republic appears to one who is still haunted by the awesome symbols of monarchy! And, as we have argued previously, how uninspiring is capitalism when compared with the heady poetry of socialism! Serendipity occurs when democratic capitalism, that most nonmythopoetic of polities, is disclosed to be the best guarantor of the deepest human aspirations and hopes. We can call this serendipity, paradox, irony. *Sub specie aeternitatis* we can also speak of grace.

Conflicting Freedoms: Individual and Collective

Raymond Duncan Gastil

INTRODUCTION: THE DEFINITION OF FREEDOMS AND THEIR LINKED DEVELOPMENT

It is a naive assumption that human rights are simple goods which can be endlessly piled one on top of another without conflict. As long as rights were few and were poorly observed in most of the world, conflicts among rights may not have seemed apparent. But rights are like children: as their production becomes less doubtful and more secure, the dangers of their unlimited proliferation become more obvious. In particular, resolving the conflict between the freedoms of majorities and the freedoms of minorities requires placing onerous limitations on both.

Any discussion of the interrelationships among political, religious, and economic rights must begin with definition. Following the assumptions of the Comparative Survey of Freedom found in *Freedom in the World*, we may define *political rights* as those political and civil liberties often associated with the concept of modern democracy.[1] In a democracy, political rights narrowly construed are the rights of people to elect their leaders

---

1. See Raymond D. Gastil, *Freedom in the World: Political Rights and Civil Liberties, 1986-1987* (Westport, Conn.: Greenwood Press, 1987). This

or representatives, or even to directly decide through referendums on the affairs of state. These rights commonly exist on a variety of levels from the local community up to the nation-state—or, in the case of the European communities, the supra–nation-state. For these rights to have meaning, they must be buttressed by a variety of politically relevant civil rights, such as rights to freedom *of* expression, assembly, organization, and movement, and overlapping rights to freedom *from* arbitrary imprisonment, torture, execution, or exile for nonviolent political action or expression.

Religious rights may be defined as a subcategory of civil liberties. Unlike political civil liberties, they should not be seen primarily in terms of their political relevance.[2] However, rights to religious expression, organization, and assembly echo the political-civil rights of the community. The meaning of these freedoms becomes clearer if we note the particular issues for which religious rights have often been alleged in recent discussions. These include rights to proselytize among people of other religions, to use political organization and symbols to campaign actively in the political arena, to not pay taxes for religiously offensive practices (such as abortion), to not have the symbols or practices of a particular religion displayed or observed in public facilities or institutions, and to refuse national service by reason of religious faith. Quite a different "religious right," the one most emphasized in international human-rights documents, is the right not to be discriminated against in employment or other spheres of life because of religious observance or belief. These rights or "freedoms" are clearly more or less directly connected to other traditional civil liberties.

Economic rights or freedoms, on the other hand, may be defined in a manner that would make them tangential to political-civil freedoms. Some, such as the rights of employers or employees to organize or act in common to express their griev-

volume has been published annually since 1978; the surveys go back to 1973. Much of the following discussion will be based on this and other volumes in the series.

2. See George Weigel, "A Preliminary Examination of Religious Freedom," in Raymond D. Gastil, *Freedom in the World: Political Rights and Civil Liberties, 1982* (Westport, Conn.: Greenwood Press, 1982), pp. 121-41.

ances, are very close to other political-civil rights. Some, such as the rights to employment or a fair wage, would seem to be matters of social policy or need that few at this conference would wish to discuss as "freedoms." Most divergent are economic freedoms as defined by those libertarians who regard any constraints on an individual's control of his resources in personal spheres or in the marketplace to be an inadmissible denial of basic human rights.

The acceptance and definition of freedoms in all three categories grew out of the historical development of Western civilization in the last few centuries and its subsequent diffusion—by conquest, education, and communication—over most of the globe. In some periods, the development of one or another specific right or class of rights may have gotten ahead of the others, but over time they moved together. For example, in the earlier period in Europe, civil and economic liberties developed more rapidly than suffrage, but today if there is any leading sector in the development of freedom, it is that of suffrage.

These freedoms resulted from and contributed to a general breakdown of the authoritarian, top-down structure of society. In religion, the universal church broke into segments, these segments further splintered, and then came the fundamental challenge: Was the church necessary in any form? (Recent religious revivals on a broad community basis have resuscitated neither the authoritarianism nor the universalist assumptions.) In politics, the rule by a single king and court, or by a very limited class of nobles and clerics, was replaced through extension of the franchise to ever-widening circles. At the same time, the right to question the actions of one's superiors and to have this right protected by the courts became generally accepted. In economics, the stranglehold of monopoly in business through royal charters or in trade through guilds was broken, and banking and price controls were greatly eased or eliminated. Land came to be a possession that could be bought and sold like any other. Most important, in the growing context of freedom, people were allowed to participate economically in any role, regardless of background or status.

In the areas of religious and political freedom, progress

has been essentially continuous from the inception of this trend to the present. Of course, there have been significant interruptions, such as the experience with national socialism in the 1930s. But if we think of 1587, 1687, 1787, 1887, and 1987 as points of reference, we find a distinctive and cumulative trend toward freedom. Before 1787 there were no countries that could have been labeled "free" in terms of a modern survey of political and civil liberties. To label the United States "free" in the 1790s would require ignoring disqualifications by reason of race and sex, and to some extent by reason of property and religion. The United States became "free" in many ways in the nineteenth century, and during that same span, very gradually, more democracies developed. If we ignore the lack of female suffrage, we can find perhaps nine operating democracies at the turn of the century. Today there are well over fifty.[3]

However, in the economic sphere the "gains" of the process seem to have been partially arrested in the heartlands of freedom after the late nineteenth century. To some degree, unions replaced guilds as constraints on the freedoms of workers and employers, while renewed governmental activism in a variety of spheres served to limit the expression of an individual's control over his property, even if it did not lead to permanent nationalization. The "failure" of liberalism to maintain nineteenth-century economic assumptions under the guidance of increasingly free majoritarian democracy has come to be regarded as inevitable by Joseph Schumpeter and other social analysts.[4] This historical divergence implies a fundamental difference between most political and civil freedoms and libertarian economic freedoms. In what follows we will discuss the important distinction in understanding all freedoms be-

---

3. On the record of democratic progress, see Raymond D. Gastil, *Freedom in the World: Political Rights and Civil Liberties, 1984-1985* (Westport, Conn.: Greenwood Press, 1985), pp. 148-68, 257-71; and G. Bingham Powell, "Social Progress and Liberal Democracy," in Gabriel Almond, Martin Chodorow, and Roy Harvey Pearce, *Progress and Its Discontents* (Berkeley and Los Angeles: University of California Press, 1982), pp. 375-402.

4. Schumpeter, *Capitalism, Socialism, and Democracy*, 2nd ed. (New York: Harper, 1947).

tween the freedom of the individual as an individual and as a member of a collectivity. The particularly heavy impact of this distinction in the economic arena may account for the historical divergence of economic freedoms from other freedoms.

INTERRELATIONSHIPS AND CAUSATION

That the freedoms with which we are concerned began developing together and for two centuries progressed together is a historical fact from which we should not draw too many conclusions. Insofar as we are talking about the same kinds of rights or freedoms, such as the economic right to organize and the political right to organize, or the religious right to free expression and the political right to free expression, they are tautologically very closely correlated rights. Perusal of the "Country Summaries" in the Comparative Survey of Freedom seldom reveals glaring anomalies in the granting or withholding of most political-civil or religious rights.

There is no clear explanation for the success of these freedoms as a group during the last few centuries. As I see it, the political organization of most peoples since the most primitive days has been largely in the hands of small minorities of recent conquerors—a situation that has produced, with depressing regularity, extreme class differences and cultures of expected repression. In recent centuries, it was only when the idea of the nation-state developed and when nation-states attained some stability that a context was provided for the growth of democratic ideas. The expansion of these ideas ideologically and internationally was probably immanent in the ideas themselves, just as the development of a literate world was immanent in the first hieroglyphs. The developing culture of democracy and equality, of respect for the individual, is innately attractive. This is not to deny that democratic culture also has weak points that can be exploited to block its expansion and bring it down.

The Comparative Survey of Freedom suggests that the intensity and/or extent of contact with the countries in the heartlands of these freedoms—Western Europe and North America—is the most likely explanation for the presence or absence of such freedoms in other parts of the world. For example, the freedoms with which we are concerned are least developed and most poorly secured in Africa: this is also the continent whose peoples have had the shortest and most tenuous contact with the West. We often forget that in much of Africa, colonialism lasted less than a century. Liberal freedoms are also little developed where they have been forcibly beaten back by intense ideological systems such as Islam or Marxism-Leninism. Other explanations for the presence or absence of such freedoms in terms of sociological or economic variables seem less compelling despite correlations that have been made.

Today, outside of parts of the Islamic world, where a fierce rearguard action is still being fought, the spread of political, civil, and economic freedoms is continuing. Belatedly, the liberal economic freedoms of the market economists have spread even to the Marxist-Leninist world. This spread has accompanied an increasingly pragmatic attitude on the part of elites, a change that is bound to accompany an aging of ideology, an aging that has long since affected the Western world. Economic reforms under Marxist-Leninist regimes do not yet imply—although by association they might bring—the political, civil, and religious freedoms that we cherish.

It has often been argued that economic freedoms of the libertarian sort are necessary for the development or sustenance of political and religious freedoms. It is certainly true that for at least two centuries the development of individual economic freedom was associated with the growth of freedom in general, as was pointed out previously. However, reflection will suggest that the relationship is tenuous at best. It is plausible to argue that general political and civil freedoms are dependent on the development of economic freedom, but the graveyard of social science is littered with plausible arguments.

The table in the Comparative Survey that compares economic and political systems has often been used as evidence of the relation of political freedom to economic freedom, despite my disclaimers.[5] The table certainly seems to show that

---

5. See the Table of Political-Economic Systems in any edition of *Freedom in the World*.

capitalism is a necessary but not sufficient condition for political and civil freedoms. But the associations appear to be due more to historical fellow traveling than to any necessary connection. In the 1980s, mainland China at times offered an opening to private initiative and a private market in many parts of its economic system, a development that has been foreshadowed in the communist world by Hungary and Yugoslavia. This does not mean, however, that political and civil freedoms as we know them will necessarily develop.

Let me qualify the last statement in two respects. First, since a totally closed society such as North Korea cannot participate in world markets, it is able to maintain a centralized command economy with little additional cost. Given its present economic policies, such closure would be impossible for China; to this extent, more civil freedoms, of an effective but unsecured quality, are likely to develop as the Chinese experiment progresses. Second, and more important, what the Chinese are doing is borrowing, as the Japanese did before them, from the successful societies of the West. History shows that once extensive borrowing is underway, it is very difficult for a society to pick and choose. Chinese educated in the West or in Western educated traditions are bound to come to demand the freedoms of the West, and leaders are eventually likely to think that they should grant such rights—even against their own self-interest. Significantly, developing the new Chinese economy was accompanied by opening long-closed churches. Opening the churches seemed fitting—psychologically and culturally—and it might improve relations with a Christian West. So I look to the changes taking place in the communist world with great hope, but my hope is not founded on the belief that there is an inevitable relationship between economic and other freedoms.

Classical market economies and individual economic freedom can thrive in countries that deny other basic civil and religious rights. To take a current example, the Ayatollah Khomeini came to power with the support of the bazaari class in Iran. The bazaaris are merchants and small manufacturers or craftsmen and have since the time of Muhammad been the main supporters of the Islamic clergy. This support explains the fact that the arena of Iranian life in which there has been, and continues to be, the most open discussion is that of economic policy, even though Khomeini weighed in on the side of the free marketers against the more socialist mullahs.[6] (Of course, the capitalism of this class is not thoroughly modern capitalism, but then the capitalism that historically formed the basis of the discussion of these issues in the past was hardly modern. If one is to demand that capitalism be that of the transnationals in the 1980s, then it is easy enough and rather pointless to say that it correlates with democracy—for the First World is both capitalist and democratic in ways that correlate precisely.)

Certainly, international or transnational capitalism today does not automatically give direct support to democracy. International capitalists support predictability and abhor political change. If democracy can give stability, fine. If a Chilean dictator or a South African racist or a Middle Eastern king can guarantee stability, fine. Capitalists and capitalism played a mixed role in Hitler's rise to power in Germany: essentially it was the role that the transnationals play in the world, a by-product of the search for a secure business environment. Transnational business may help to transmit Western values and to open up societies to influences from the democratic heartland; in this indirect sense transnationals aid democratic development.

Looking at the problem from the opposite end of the telescope, it is hard to show that curtailing economic individualism has threatened political or religious freedom. The economic controls of varying extensiveness that have been implemented at various times in Western Europe—in countries such as the United Kingdom or Sweden—since World War II have not mortally threatened democracy or made impossible reversals in the centralization of economic power. It might seem that the heavy bureaucratization of the United Kingdom, along with nationalization and the destruction of private medicine, would have harmed non-economic freedoms by reducing pluralism, but I see little evidence of this effect.

Hong Kong illustrates the fact that religious and economic

---

6. A review of the English language section of *Iran Times*, a Washington weekly, would provide the best evidence of this continuing story.

freedoms can thrive without the normal majoritarian political freedoms. Hong Kong does without political freedoms because of the special relationship between the British administration and communist China, but civil liberties have nevertheless been well secured. Fewer civil liberties but more political freedoms have characterized the comparable societies of Singapore, South Korea, and Taiwan.

The recent history of Japan casts considerable doubt on the association of economic freedom, economic development, and political and religious freedom. Since the Meiji Restoration, Japan has tried to copy Western institutions under the paternalistic control of its political-economic elite. In this process, business has thrived, and development has been steady and impressive, regardless of the political and civil-rights regimes in power. Since the end of World War II, with the strain of supporting a large defense establishment lifted from their shoulders, the Japanese have combined this growth with an effective system of political, economic, religious, and civil liberties. But the steady trend of the Japanese accomplishment suggests that even without Western freedoms, the growth would have proceeded apace, and the economic system would not have been greatly different than it is today.

THE CONFLICT OF INDIVIDUAL AND COLLECTIVE FREEDOM

A major challenge for the West and for Western intellectuals is to understand and accept the conflicts within the concept of freedom before these conflicts issue in new threats against the core institutions of freedom. In particular, we need to understand and make peace with those conflicts that emerge from the fact that freedoms refer both to collective freedoms *and* to individual freedoms.

Let me introduce the point with a short story. Imagine an island with ten people on it, and imagine that all these people have decided to leave the island. Some want to build an airplane as a means of departure; others want to build a boat. It is generally agreed that all the surplus for the next year, until the hurricanes come, must be spent on either a boat or an airplane. To divide the surplus and try to build both will mean the failure of both projects. To solve the problem, the group decides on a referendum. Six vote to build a boat, and four vote to build an airplane. Of course, if a boat is built with the surplus of all ten, then in a sense the four will be oppressed—all their surplus will be taxed away to build a boat they do not want. Yet if a boat is not built, nothing will be done, and the six will also not achieve their objectives. As I see it, this would be the greater oppression.

The essence of political freedom is that every individual has an equal right to participate in those decisions which require that a group decision rather than an individual decision be made. Equal political rights means that in such decisions each person has an equal share; the most practical expression of this equality is majority rule. I make these rather obvious comments because when I presented this story at a small conference of conservative/libertarian economists last year, almost everyone in the room rejected my conclusion. They judged building a boat with the help of taxes on the four to be oppressive, and proposed any number of other alternatives to such "majority tyranny." Some preferred a lottery; others would have had the group strive for consensus. I am afraid that their objections were as incomprehensible to me as my majoritarianism appeared outrageous to them.

Freedom is attained by a society only when it balances the rights of majorities and minorities, and grants to each what is properly its share. Any free society will grant minorities—ultimately individuals—certain rights that cannot be taken away from them without destroying the freedom of all. The rights of free, rational speech, organization, and assembly are included among these, for informed majority choice is possible only in the presence of such rights. To put it differently, only through free speech can opinions be restructured to make possible new majorities around new topics. This is key: I believe that what ultimately may make majorities of the moment bearable for members of the minority is the chance for new majorities to develop and for particular individuals to be in majorities and minorities on different issues. Another basic right of the minority is access to a fair and dependable legal system. But whatever we include in these basic rights, we must strive to keep the list of minority guarantees short. We must not forget that every right which a minority is given in our search for balanced freedom takes rights away from the majority—or, to put it differently, it diminishes the ability of the individuals who generally make up the majority to build or preserve the society that they desire.

Parenthetically, the reader should note that in making this distinction, I am not distinguishing between individual and "group" rights in the sense of the rights of religious or ethnic minorities. Such minorities have rights analogous to those we are discussing here, but the existence of such rights is not an obvious extrapolation from the foregoing discussion, which is based on separating and adding together autonomous individuals of equal legal status, regardless of the affiliations that are conventionally ascribed to them.

In the political arena, we should notice that the granting of rights to local communities restricts the rights of the larger community. The United States might end up without a nuclear power industry because the states and communities that could reasonably be expected to house waste repositories (because of low population density and acceptable geology) refuse to accept them. Those refusing to allow sites might be small in number, but their power in this regard could be overwhelming. As a nation we might accept this outcome, because on other issues other communities would also want to have the final word. Such politics effectively tie the hands of national leaders to implement policies, approved by the majority in this and other policy areas. To take another example, the majority in one of the fifty states might pass a strong, well-written anti-pornography law. Yet the courts might use the First Amendment as a basis for declaring the law inoperative—in defense of the minority rights of those who want continued access to pornography. I am not saying what is right or wrong in these examples, but merely pointing out the "costs" to the majority of guaranteeing minority rights.

Religious freedom must be understood analogously in terms of a conflict between the rights of the majority and the rights of the minority. Insofar as religion is important to a population, those in the majority are likely to want their local and national communities to express significant aspects of religious life as they understand it. In accepting this proposition, we must remember that the claims of religion in the minds of many are very broad indeed. They stretch from private and public belief and worship into the realms of art, family life, economics, and beyond. The traditionally religious could hardly be expected to accept the idea that a majority religious community could not determine minimum standards of public dress and behavior. Indeed, a major problem with understanding religious freedom is understanding the limits we are to put on "religion"—and who else should decide these limits but the majority itself?

For example, today the United States finds itself confronted with massive public disputes over abortion, both the right of individuals to have or perform an abortion and the right of majorities to deny the use of their money to support abortions here and abroad. Clearly, if the rights of the majority to affect this issue are constrained by concern for minority or individual rights (or the rights of peoples outside the community), then the majority is to that degree deprived of political freedom.

Freedom for a minority or an individual to proselytize is obviously central to the question of religious freedom. This is a right freely granted in most modern democracies, although more freely in some than in others. In developing democracies such as India and in most of the Third World, it is a right generally restricted. Similarly, in such societies individuals are often forbidden to engage in practices or kinds of expression that offend the majority's sense of the sacred—that is why the killing of cattle has been restricted in India. In legislating such prohibitions, the majority community makes at least three claims. First, it is offensive to their religious sensibilities to have their religion attacked, directly or indirectly, by preachers of other faiths. Second, the people in the community have a right to assume that their children will be brought up within the same religious traditions that they themselves were. Third, the majority community has a right not to have its religious sensibilities ignored by the public acts of others. In a society in which religion is held as the highest value, people find it hard to understand why a majority cannot use its vote to defend such religious values.

Closer to our own world, many communities have lately found that they can no longer allow as a community or allow on community property the public showing of religious symbols, particularly at Christmastime. In the American tradition this stems from insistence on the separation of church and state, a doctrine that has served the country well. Yet such rules or decisions restrict the communal expression of the overwhelming majority. It seems to me that in this case the rights of a minority of disbelievers or other-believers are given undue precedence over the rights of a majority to use their "commons" as they see fit. Restrictions on school prayer, on the other hand, would seem to have more justification, because in the psychologically coercive atmosphere of a classroom, the minority student might be put under undue pressure to conform and thus ultimately to change his beliefs to fit those of his fellow students. The distinction is perhaps between the passive and active expression of the religious majority.

THE SPECIAL PROBLEM OF MINORITY ECONOMIC FREEDOM

Economic freedom should also be understood as a two-sided freedom of the majority and the minority. When a colleague and I set out a few years ago to generate a definition of economic freedom, we developed an essentially mixed definition.[7] Central to our concept is the idea that political rights are primary. In other words, unlike my friends at the conference I referred to previously, we believe that a community has a right to freely arrive at a definition of the kind of economic system it wants, and to change that system as experience accumulates. We propose, in other words, that economic freedom is primarily the freedom of the collectivity. Many

---

7. See Lindsay M. Wright, "A Comparative Survey of Economic Freedoms," in Raymond D. Gastil, *Freedom in the World, 1982,* pp. 51-90, as well as the Table of Economic Freedom in the 1983-1984 edition (Westport, Conn.: Greenwood Press, 1984), pp. 40-41. See also *Freedom in the World, 1984-1985,* pp. 169, 178. This latter is the first edition in which we fully expressed the tension between individual and collective rights.

economists will assert, and with good evidence, that if a community assumes that this means that it should directly operate the economy through governmental bureaucracies, this will lead to gross inefficiencies. But this is a practical matter. It is up to the voters to decide in terms of their values the balance of public and private ownership, of regulation and lack of regulation. As long as an economic system does not through its own operation compel an undue endorsement of itself by the voters—although to a degree all economic systems will be conservative and self-affirming through the ballot box—it preserves the openness to change that is at the heart of democratic, majoritarian freedom.

It is less clear what the equivalent "minimum conditions of economic freedom" for the minority might be that would be equivalent to the minimum conditions for political and religious freedom sketched previously. The fact that many democracies have instigated a compulsory draft for military service, sometimes even in peacetime, suggests that democratic majorities have assumed they have an almost unlimited right to the service and even the lives of their fellow citizens, should the need be severe enough. (I wonder if they have this right—certainly many of my libertarian friends deny that they do.) The acceptance under many conditions of price controls, including rent controls, and minimum wage laws implies that democratic majorities believe their fellow citizens do not have the right to offer their services or products at rates which they might individually desire.

Thus, it seems to be the case that while many economists and libertarians are willing to proclaim absolute economic rights for individuals from an individualistic and what I think is a quite unrealistic perspective, in practice these rights have been regularly denied by card-carrying democrats. The fact that these denials have not been anywhere near as broad and disturbing in other areas of civil freedom, such as those of religion and free speech, suggests that in democracies economic freedom is not understood in the way that libertarian economists understand it. There are good practical reasons for this rejection of absolute economic individualism. But if we deny this absolutism to individual economic rights, we are left with little guidance about where to draw the line against the total extinction of individual rights in the economic sphere.[8]

As a tentative beginning to carving out an area for such rights, one absolute right might be drawn from the fuzzy and little-developed area of privacy rights—that everyone should be able to pursue his private life, economically or otherwise, without undue interference or intrusion by others insofar as this private life does not intrude on the interests of others. Just as I should be able to turn the radio off and on as I desire (out of the hearing of others), or attend a particular church or not attend any church, I should be able to grow or not grow a garden, or save or not save stamps. From this beginning we can perhaps develop other basic economic freedoms for the minority individual, but it is unclear what they are. What is clear is that as we try to extend and define the boundaries for such rights, we must be cognizant of the historical expression of majority economic rights under a variety of conditions.

Parenthetically, there is also another class of economic, religious, and political rights that are tangentially related to freedom—rights to be free from discrimination because of race, sex, or ethnicity. I find that such "freedoms," however desirable, do not fit comfortably with the other freedoms we are discussing here. They could, in fact, be thoroughly respected in a totally unfree society such as North Korea, which was not concerned with such distinctions.

CONCLUSION

We may conclude that political, religious, and economic freedom are interrelated definitionally, and that all rest on a society's willingness to identify the individual as the ultimate human value, as the ultimate unit of decision in both individual

---

8. I find discussions such as those of John Rawls in *A Theory of Justice* (Cambridge: Belknap Press, 1971) and Robert Nozick in *Anarchy, State, and Utopia* (New York: Basic Books, 1974) interesting theoretically but of little practical use in defining those basic individual economic rights without which a society cannot be considered free.

and group life. This implies a decision-making system that allows all citizens to take an equal part in the political process through referendums, the election of representatives, or even representation through citizens chosen temporarily by lot, as in ancient Athens or our present jury system. It also involves a balancing of individual and collective freedoms, a balancing performed in the political arena through the distinction of political and civil liberties, and more problematically in the religious arena through the separation of church and state in the American tradition. Most religious minority rights in most states are protected essentially by an extension of generally recognized political and private civil liberties. In theory, how this balance should be achieved in the economic arena through analogy to civil liberties is less clear. However, in the real democratic world, the balance of political forces and traditions as well as pragmatic considerations is likely to preserve a considerable area of individual economic freedom.

Political, religious, and economic freedoms should be seen, then, as closely related in their origin, but their relationship is cultural, historical, and intrinsic rather than sociological. All three freedoms offer potentially conflictful rights to citizens both as individuals and as members of political communities. Establishing a balance between majority and minority freedoms is particularly difficult in the economic arena, because the ground rules for basic individual rights have not been worked out or accepted in practice. Developing practical minimums for freedom in this sphere, rather than engaging in ideological struggles to disenfranchise majorities, is a principal requirement for the further institutionalization of freedom.

Religious Freedom:
The First Human Right

George Weigel

As one surveys the rhetoric of human rights in both international and domestic public life today, one cannot but be struck by the amount of special pleading that goes on in the name of the "priority" of this, that, or the other putative "human right." In our own domestic politics, things have gone so far that the "right to abortion" was asserted, by some combatants in the debate over Judge Robert Bork's nomination to the U.S. Supreme Court, as the most fundamental personal guarantee under the Constitution of 1787.

We know, I hope, that there is something quite wrong, conceptually and practically, with the use of rights language as a rhetorical intensifier in partisan political debate. Yet most thoughtful people also understand that there is a hierarchy of values in the field of human rights. We know intuitively that free speech is a more fundamental human right than the "right" to a jury trial in a civil law suit. We know intuitively that *habeas corpus* is a more crucial guarantor of individual liberty than the putative "right" to a secondary education. Little reflection is required to recognize that, even among people of goodwill and liberal instincts (and still more in the face of the modern assault on human rights by authoritarian and totalitarian regimes), there is a job of sorting out to be done here.

But the issues involved in thinking through a hierarchy

of human rights are more than issues of conceptual propriety. They bear as well on the question of the structure of freedom, which is the special concern of this conference. Can one make the case that some human rights, if actualized in public life, are the condition for the possibility of the honoring of other human rights? Put even more sharply, is there one radically basic human right, the acknowledgment of which, in theory and in practice, is the irreducible foundation, the *sine qua non*, of any meaningful scheme of "human rights"?

With due respect for the dangers of special pleading in this complex and volatile field, I shall argue in this essay that there is, in theory and in practice, one absolutely fundamental human right: the right of religious freedom or, more broadly put, freedom of conscience. I will put the argument on behalf of this claim in propositional form to facilitate argument and refinement, and I will follow it with two more discursive sections exploring the notion that religious freedom is indeed the first of human rights.

I. RELIGIOUS FREEDOM AND THE HUMAN PERSON: THE INTERIOR MEANING OF RELIGIOUS FREEDOM

1. Human beings are more than individuals; human beings are persons distinguished by an innate capacity for thinking, choosing, and acting, and by an innate drive for meaning and value.

Whether one proceeds anthropologically, phenomenologically, sociologically, or theologically, there would seem to be broad agreement that *the* distinguishing characteristic of human beings as contrasted with other forms of sensate life is our unquenchable desire to know who we are and what our place is in the order of things, and to organize our world according to those understandings. Intellect and will are thus not epiphenomenal, the expression of other mundane forces (e.g., economic forces). Intellect and will are built into the very structure of human being in the world; they are the fundamental, defining characteristics of a human being. Recognition of these constitutive dimensions of personhood does not re-

quire— although it may indeed be supported by—adherence
to what believers would understand as religious revelation.

> 2. *Freedom to pursue the quest for meaning and value, without
> coercion, is a fundamental dynamic of human being in the
> world.*

When one speaks of "human dignity," one often thinks of the
material necessities of life: food, clothing, shelter, and so forth.
Yet we know from our own personal experience as well as from
human history that the satisfaction of these material needs does
not exhaust the meaning of "human dignity." Were that the case,
there would be no essential difference between human beings
and other forms of sensate life. The biblical claim that "Man does
not live by bread alone" is understood and affirmed far beyond
the limits of the Jewish and Christian religious communities. In
modern times we know, for example, of societies in which the
provision of material goods is reasonably adequate—people are
not starving, there is adequate medical care, children do not run
the streets naked—but in which the fullness of "human dignity"
is sorely lacking and is understood to be lacking by the fact that
people persistently try to leave those societies (and their over-
seers persistently try to prevent that from happening). Some
advanced industrialized states of the Marxist-Leninist "Second
World" are the most obvious empirical examples. In these states,
what we can term (following Pope John Paul II) the "interior
freedom" of the human person is being violated.

> 3. *This innate human quest for meaning and value, which is
> the basic dynamic of the "interior freedom" of the human per-
> son, is the end or object of that "human right" which we refer
> to as the "right of religious freedom" or "freedom of conscience."*

Religious freedom or freedom of conscience is thus not a
"grant" from the state or from society. Human beings are to
enjoy the free and unfettered pursuit of truth because they are
human beings and because the denial of that pursuit is, in the
deepest meaning of the term, "inhuman." When we refer to the
"right" of religious freedom or freedom of conscience, we are

referring to a juridical expression of this basic claim about the essential core and dynamic of human being in the world.

4. Thus religious freedom or freedom of conscience is the most fundamental of human rights.

It is most fundamental because it is that right or claim which corresponds to the most radically (that is, fundamentally) human dimension of human being in the world. When religious freedom or freedom of conscience is absent, human beings lack not merely one of the many goods to be sought in life. To deny or obstruct religious freedom or freedom of conscience is to do violence to the very structure of human being in the world, to deny the constitutive elements of personhood.

5. The right of religious freedom was defined with precision by the Second Vatican Council in Dignitatis Humanae Personae (The Declaration on Religious Freedom): *"The human person has a right to religious freedom. This freedom means that all men are to be immune from coercion on the part of individuals or of social groups and of any human power, in such wise that in matters religious no one is to be forced to act in a manner contrary to his beliefs. Nor is anyone to be restrained from acting in accordance with his own beliefs, whether privately or publicly, whether alone or in association with others, within due limits."*

This definition contains several important claims. First, it defines religious freedom as an issue involving the essence of the human person. Second, it acknowledges the privileges of conscience both for religious believers and for non-believers; religious belief is not to be coerced, nor should it involve civil penalties for believers. Third, religious belief (or unbelief) is a *public* matter; men are to be free to *act* on their conscientious convictions, provided, as the Council put it, "that the just requirements of public order are observed." Fourth, the Conciliar definition suggests that the right of religious freedom involves a concomitant obligation to pursue the truth and a civic responsibility to see that the pursuit of truth can be publicly engaged and contested.

The right of religious freedom therefore involves, of its very nature, the right to the public profession of religious conviction, individually and communally, and, *ceteris paribus*, the right to be immune from coerced public religious profession or practice. Thus public argument for or against religious conviction, the public celebration *(liturgia)* of religious conviction (or one's conscientious abstinence therefrom), the transmission of religious belief to one's children (or the immunity of one's children from such instruction), and the establishment of organizations and institutions that are expressions of religious conviction (e.g., institutions of education and charity or social service) are matters of individual conscientious decision or of the decision of those communities that form around matters of conscientious conviction, not matters of state policy or social coercion in any form—again, of course, consonant with the requirements of public order.

> 6. *Religious freedom or freedom of conscience can thus be considered a "pre-political" human right: religious freedom or freedom of conscience is the condition for the possibility of a* polis *that is structured in accordance with the inherent human dignity of the persons who are its citizens.*

The *right* of religious freedom or freedom of conscience entails an *obligation* to seek the truth. Acknowledgment of the right of religious freedom therefore requires, if the right is not to be a "parchment barrier" (as Madison would have it), a structuring of society such that a de-politicized (i.e., non-coercive) search for truth is possible for individuals, privately and publicly, and such that the rights of conscience for all men and women are protected.

And here is where the "interior" meaning of religious freedom touches the "public" meaning of religious freedom or freedom of conscience.

II. RELIGIOUS FREEDOM AND THE STRUCTURE OF FREEDOM IN THE WORLD: THE PUBLIC MEANING OF RELIGIOUS FREEDOM

7. The right of religious freedom establishes a fundamental barrier or distinction between the person and the state which is essential in any true polis.

While the right of religious freedom, in one form or another, has been asserted for centuries, it is no accident that this right has been most forcefully claimed, and indeed codified in international law, in the century of totalitarianism. Whether or not totalitarian states effectively control all aspects of human life, the fact remains that that is their declared intention, as Hannah Arendt and others have argued in defining the distinctiveness of the totalitarian project over against traditional despotisms or "authoritarianisms." The right of religious freedom, conversely, is a declaration that there is an inviolable sanctuary of conscience (a *sanctum sanctorum,* if you will) at the center of the human person, a sanctuary into which the coercive power of the state may not tread. States that do so tread are, by their very nature, oppressors in the most radical or fundamental sense. As Peter Berger argues in the first essay in this volume, "religious liberty is fundamental because it posits the ultimate limit on the power of the state." The state may not, in other words, violate that most basic of human prerogatives: the prerogative of determining and acting upon one's conscientious convictions about those matters that are most radically human—those matters that engage what Berger calls the "transcendent intentionality" of human persons and communities. Thus religion, to cite Berger again, "relativizes, puts in proper place, all the realities of this world, including all institutions." Religious conviction—indeed, conscientious human conviction that appeals to genuinely transcendent warrants (as in the case of, say, Sidney Hook)—establishes the penultimacy of the political.

8. The right of religious freedom is a crucial component in establishing that distinction between "society" and the "state" which is fundamental to the democratic project.

While the right of religious freedom or freedom of conscience can be acknowledged and observed in a modern authoritarian state (e.g., the Philippines of Ferdinand Marcos), the empirical fact seems to be that religious freedom is most regularly safeguarded in democracies. That is so because democracies recognize—indeed, are founded upon—the concept of free persons constituting a free people under a limited state. Whether one traces the roots of modern democratic theory and practice to the English, Scottish, and/or French Enlightenment, or whether one finds democracy's deeper taproots in Puritan understandings ("The poorest he that is in England hath a life to live as the greatest he," as Colonel Rainsborough put it), in Christian medieval political theory (with its notion of the people's "inherent sense of justice," and its claim that the good prince rules by consent rather than by sheer coercion), and/or in classic Greek political philosophy and Roman law, the fact remains that democracy, in theory and in practice, is built upon the distinction between society and the state, upon the claim that society is prior to the state, and upon the understanding that the state exists to serve society, not the other way around. Social institutions, in other words, have a logical, historical, and, one might even say, "ontological" priority over the institutions of government.

And among the most persistent of the social institutions that have claimed this priority in the West are religious institutions, specifically the Christian church. When Pope Gelasius I informed the Byzantine Emperor Anastasius I in A.D. 494 that "two there are, august emperor, by which this world is ruled on title of original and sovereign right—the consecrated authority of the priesthood and the royal power," he was rejecting any monistic (or, in modern terms, "totalitarian") view of human society and polity. Gelasius I would not, of course, have argued the case for religious freedom on the personalist grounds suggested in Part I of this essay; and his successors in the Christian community, Catholic and Protestant, were to honor this basic distinction perhaps more in the breach than in the observance at many points in Western history. But in this "Gelasian tradition" we may find, in ancient form, the basis of a rejection of totalitarian claims and, conversely, the root of those political understandings which, through a complex path, eventually gave birth in the West to the democratic project.

> 9. *The priority of religious freedom in any meaningful scheme*
> *of "human rights" is empirically confirmed, in modern times,*
> *by the totalitarian attack on religious belief and practice.*

It is no accident, as Marxists might say, that totalitarian regimes—and particularly Leninist totalitarian regimes—have put such ferocious efforts into the oppression of religious believers and institutions. Lenin understood, in a way that Marx did not, that the totalitarian project of constructing the "new man" was most fundamentally threatened by religion. Thus the function of ideology in a totalitarian state is to effect a radical social control, a perverted anti-transcendence to replace the transcendent horizon against which the society in question had once lived; the hammer and sickle constitute, if you will, a crippled cross.

In *Modern Times*, Paul Johnson captured this dimension of the Leninist enterprise well:

> Religion was important to [Lenin] in the sense that he hated it. Unlike Marx, who despised it and treated it as marginal, Lenin saw it as a powerful and ubiquitous enemy. . . . "There can be nothing more abominable," he wrote, "than religion." From the start, the state he created set up and maintains to this day an enormous academic propaganda machine against religion. . . . Lenin had no feelings about corrupt priests, because they were easily beaten. The men he really feared and hated, and later persecuted, were the saints. The purer the religion, the more dangerous. . . . The clergy most in need of suppression were not those committed to the defense of exploitation but those who expressed their solidarity with the proletariat and the peasants. It was as though he recognized in the true man of God the same

zeal and spirit which animated himself, and wished to expropriate it and enlist it in his own cause.[1]

Lenin's approach to religion in the working out of the totalitarian project has been refined by his self-proclaimed heirs; the most popular instrument among those with Leninist ambitions today seems to be not so much a frontal assault on religious institutions but rather the establishment of parallel pseudo-religious institutions under state control (e.g., the *Pacem in Terris* organization in Czechoslovakia; the "popular church" in Nicaragua). But whatever the tactics chosen, it is precisely totalitarians who perhaps most intuitively understand the priority of religious freedom and the consequent, antipathetic relationship between religious freedom and their own designs for political power. For the state that acknowledges and honors the right of religious freedom or freedom of conscience is the state that acknowledges its own limits. Thus, and parenthetically, one could argue that the most radical test of the *glasnost* and *perestroika* of Mikhail Gorbachev will be precisely on the question of the relationship between the Soviet state and religious believers and religious institutions.

10. Democracies protect religious freedom; yet the relationship also cuts the other way—religious freedom is a fundamental guarantor of democracy.

This can be argued in two ways. In the first instance, the right of religious freedom or freedom of conscience, asserted in theory and observed in practice, helps create the conditions for the possibility of addressing the threat of the Jacobinic tyranny of the majority, or what some have called "totalitarian democracy." For the right of religious freedom is asserted against democratic majorities that would use coercion in the matter of fundamental human conscientious conviction just as much as it is asserted against the claims of true totalitarians. The threat of Jacobinism is diminished to precisely the degree

---

1. Johnson, *Modern Times: The World from the Twenties to the Eighties* (New York: Harper & Row, 1983), pp. 50-51.

to which religious freedom or freedom of conscience is observed in practice and not merely bowed to in public rhetoric.

Thus democracies themselves must tread with extreme care in the arena of public policy when issues that involve religious conviction are engaged. (The American experiences with the questions of conscientious objection to military service and with the questions of education for Amish children come immediately to mind.) The requirements of public order are a limiting factor here; but the boundaries by which the society determines what religious practices gravely threaten civil unity or peace should be drawn as widely as possible—not only on humanitarian grounds, but precisely for the sake of honoring those commitments which are the fundamental building-blocks of democracy itself.

In the second instance, religious freedom, and particularly the free expression of religious conviction and the moral understandings that flow therefrom in public debate over the right ordering of society, may well be important factors in addressing what Peter Berger in his essay describes as the "serendipity" of liberty. Democratic politics is not a matter of procedure alone. The democratic experiment—and democracy is always an experiment, a never-to-be-completed test of the capacities of human beings for self-government—requires certain habits (virtues) and attitudes as well as the more familiar ensemble of democratic procedures (e.g., separation of powers, elections by secret ballot, legal protection for defeated political parties or candidates, universal enfranchisement, etc.). While the state itself has a measure of responsibility for inculcating democratic values and attitudes (cf. the statement entitled "Education for Democracy," issued by the American Federation of Teachers), experience seems to suggest that democratic "habits" are most effectively nurtured by the "prior" institutions of the society, including most particularly the family and religious institutions. This seems to be the case in contemporary America, where democratic habits and commitments are intimately related to Jewish and Christian religious convictions as those are transmitted by parents and by religious institutions, and where the warrants that the majority cite in support of democracy at home and abroad have Judeo-Christian roots, not Enlightenment-philosophical roots, as Richard John Neuhaus has argued in *The Naked Public Square*. Religious freedom, at least as exercised in the United States and other Western democracies, thus seems to result in the cultivation of those political commitments required so that the life of liberty and its expression in free institutions of governance is less "serendipitous" and more deeply and permanently grounded in the convictions of the people in whose name democratic political leaders claim to exercise public authority.

11. The right relationship between religious freedom and the democratic project is best achieved in practice when there is no state "establishment" of religion.

It is true that the right of religious freedom or freedom of conscience is honored in democratic societies that have established or "state" religious institutions, such as the United Kingdom. But there are two reasons to be concerned about this mode of arranging the relationship between religious and political affairs.

In the first place, religious institutions tend to suffer, to weaken and atrophy, when they are "kept" institutions. The vigor of the Roman Catholic Church in Poland (and, indeed, the vigor of Catholicism and other religious bodies under "disestablishment" in the United States) may be contrasted here to the sclerotic condition of the Church of England in the United Kingdom. The latter circumstance has numerous causes, but it would seem unlikely that there is no causal connection whatsoever between the Church of England's "establishment" and its current moribund state. One could also cite in this regard the weakened situation of those Christian communities in Western Europe that receive state benefices (e.g., clergy salaries), as contrasted with the vigorous life of Christian communities in Africa or Latin America. Disestablishment, it seems, is good for religion, and in any event seems more congruent with the claims involved in the concept of religious freedom (in both its "interior" and "public" meanings) sketched previously.

Disestablishment is also good for democracy. Establishment blurs, unnecessarily, the boundaries between state and society. And as these boundaries are an important constitutive element in democratic theory and practice, the blurring of them in some fashion weakens the democratic project—perhaps not fatally, but the potential for unnecessary damage is there. The desacralizing of politics, which is (as argued previously) an important political corollary of the right of religious freedom as well as a fundamental conceptual building-block of democratic theory and practice, is impeded when politics enters the realm of the sanctuary and political leaders exercise specific functions within religious institutions. When this happens, politics is no longer seen as penultimate. And thus prime ministers who appoint bishops do a measure of damage to their own office as well as to the office of bishop.

In terms of both democratic theory and the right of religious freedom, disestablishment ought to serve the cause of the free exercise of religion, as Richard Neuhaus and others have argued. Would American constitutional theory and Supreme Court jurisprudence be in a less chaotic condition today had the framers added but one word to the First Amendment, so that it read "Congress shall make no law providing for an establishment of religion, or *otherwise* prohibiting the free exercise thereof"? The specific point is moot, of course, but the larger point remains: disestablishment is to the advantage of both church and state, to the cause of religious freedom as well as to the functioning of democratic polities.

Disestablishment does not, however, require utter and radical separation between religious institutions and state institutions or between religiously based values and public debate over the right ordering of society, as envisioned in our own time by, say, People for the American Way. If a recognized social good and public obligation (e.g., the education of children or the care of the elderly or the orphaned) is being pursued, it would seem to make no *essential* difference (to either religious freedom or democracy) if public funds to achieve those social goods are channeled through religiously based or operated institutions (the effects of such funding on the charitable instincts of religious individuals and institutions are another matter). Nor should disestablishment be taken to mean that religiously based values are *ipso facto* ruled out of bounds in public policy discourse. (The prudential wisdom of appeal to religious warrants in a pluralistic society is a different, albeit related, issue.) Here, however, we are into deep waters that are beyond the scope of this essay, and the reader is referred to Neuhaus's *Naked Public Square* for an argument congruent with that being sketched here.

III. THE PRIORITY OF RELIGIOUS FREEDOM IN THE THOUGHT OF JOHN PAUL II

One of the more notable developments in the modern history of the debate over religious freedom has been the vigorous role played by the Roman Catholic Church as a principled advocate for the right of religious freedom or freedom of conscience. I say "notable" in that the teaching of the magisterium of the Catholic Church through the 1950s held to what was referred to as the "thesis/hypothesis" view of religious freedom and of church-state issues in general. In that view, expounded most forcefully in the 1940s and 1950s by the late Cardinal Alfredo Ottaviani, the "thesis," or preferred arrangement, was the confessional state in which the Catholic Church would have not only cultural pride of place but also the active support of the civil authorities; Francoist Spain was considered one expression of this arrangement. Against it, the Catholic Church would tolerate, by reason of historical necessity, the "hypothesis" arrangement of a confessionally neutral state (as in the United States) or the establishment of another Christian faith by state authorities (as in the United Kingdom or Sweden, for example). But under these latter arrangements, one public task of the Catholic Church was understood to be to work for the day when the "thesis" arrangement would prevail. In simplest form, the moral claim undergirding Ottaviani's formula was that "error has no rights," while its ecclesiological basis was the notion that the Catholic Church was the one and only true Church of Christ.

The challenge to Ottaviani's view mounted by the American Jesuit John Courtney Murray in the late 1940s and early 1950s (a challenge that, in its original form, drew on even as it extended the late-nineteenth-century church-state theory of Pope Leo XIII) eventually prevailed at the Second Vatican Council. The key shift in the argument was from what one might term Ottaviani's purely juridical view of "rights" to Murray's more personalist framing of the issue. The question, Murray argued, was not whether "error" has "rights." *Persons* have rights, and the right of religious freedom or freedom of conscience is among the foremost of these. This was the teaching adopted by Vatican II in *Dignitatis Humanae Personae (The Declaration on Religious Freedom)* cited previously.

The Council's declaration dealt with what I have previously called in this essay the "interior" meaning of the right of religious freedom, and when questions of the civic order were engaged, the declaration described religious freedom as a right against the coercive power of the state. But the Council did not devote significant attention to what I have called here the "public" meaning of religious freedom—that is, religious freedom as that basic right which, acknowledged and observed, creates one essential condition for the possibility of just governance in a rightly ordered society. This further development of the Catholic discussion has been undertaken by Pope John Paul II since his election to the chair of St. Peter in 1978.

Just as the experience of the church in the United States helped shape Murray's transformation of Catholic church-state theory such that the Council could adopt *Dignitatis Humanae Personae*, so, too, has John Paul II's experience of the Catholic Church in Poland under the heel of the two great totalitarian powers of the twentieth century shaped the most recent evolution of the Catholic argument on behalf of religious freedom. But John Paul II's defense of religious freedom begins not with history or with political theory, and still less with denominational or institutional special pleading, but with that phenomenology of the human person that is so central a component of the pope's thought. The pope begins, in other words, with a basic anthropological definition: "Man . . . is a person, that is to say a subjective being capable of acting in a planned and rational way, capable of deciding about himself and with a tendency to self-realization" (*Laborem Exercens,* 6).

This phenomenology of the person then leads to the pope's analysis of the threat posed by the violation today of the right of religious freedom:

> Man rightly fears falling victim to an oppression that will deprive him of his interior freedom, of the possibility of expressing

the truth of which he is convinced, of the faith that he professes, of the ability to obey the voice of conscience that tells him the right path to follow. The technical means at the disposal of modern society conceal within themselves not only the possibility of self-destruction through military conflict, but also the possibility of a "peaceful" subjugation of individuals, of environments, of entire societies and of nations, that for one reason or another might prove inconvenient for those who possess the necessary means and are ready to use them without scruple. . . . Together with the biological threat, therefore, there is a growing awareness of yet another threat, even more destructive of what is essentially human, what is intimately bound up with the dignity of the human person and his or her right to truth and freedom. (*Dives in Misericordia*, 11)

John Paul's description of the "interior meaning" of religious freedom then leads him to a discussion of the "public meaning" of the right of religious freedom or freedom of conscience; and here is where the pope expands the Council's discussion in *Dignitatis Humanae Personae:*

The rights of power can only be understood on the basis of respect for the objective and inviolable rights of man. The common good that authority in the State serves is brought to full realization only when all citizens are sure of their rights. The lack of this leads to the dissolution of society, opposition by citizens to authority, or a situation of oppression, intimidation, violence, and terrorism, of which many examples have been provided by the totalitarianisms of this century. Thus the principle of human rights is of profound concern to the area of social justice and is the measure by which it can be tested in the life of political bodies. . . . These rights are rightly reckoned to include the right of religious freedom together with the right to freedom of conscience. . . . Certainly the curtailment of the religious freedom of individuals and communities is not only a painful experience but it is above all an attack on man's very dignity, independently of the religion professed or of the concept of the world which these individuals or communities have. The curtailment and violation of religious freedom are in contrast with man's dignity and his objective rights. . . . [They are] a radical injustice to what is particularly deep within man, what is authentically human. (*Redemptor Hominis*, 17)

The pope's discussion of the relationship between religious freedom and the just society was further extended by the *Instruction on Christian Freedom and Liberation*, issued in March 1986 by the Congregation for the Doctrine of the Faith. The instruction was, in part, a response to those currents in the theologies of liberation that would subordinate the right of religious freedom to other putative social, economic, or political goods. In its instruction, which was issued with the pope's personal authority, the Congregation made a declaration quite to the contrary:

> There can only be authentic development in a social and political system which respects freedoms and fosters them through the participation of everyone. This participation can take many forms; it is necessary in order to guarantee a proper pluralism in institutions and in social initiatives. It ensures, notably by the real separation between the powers of the State, the exercise of human rights, also protecting them against possible abuses on the part of the public powers. No one can be excluded from this participation in social and political life for reasons of sex, race, color, social condition, language, or religion. . . . When the political authorities regulate the exercise of freedoms, they cannot use the pretext of the demands of public order and security in order to curtail those freedoms systematically. Nor can the alleged principle of national security, or a narrowly economic outlook, or a totalitarian concept of social life, prevail over the value of freedom and its rights. (*Instruction on Christian Freedom and Liberation*, 95)

Thus the pope's claim that "religious freedom . . . is the basis of all other freedoms and is inseparably tied to them all by reason of that very dignity which is the human person" (Letter to U.N. Secretary General Waldheim, 2 Dec. 1978) addresses both the "interior" and the "public" meanings of the right of religious freedom or freedom of conscience. As Father James Schall, S.J., has put it, the pope believes that "the state is legally incompetent at man's deepest levels, in his spirit, but . . . it can and ought to recognize the importance of religious values for the state's own progress."[2] Thus the pope could

---

2. Schall, *The Church, the State, and Society in the Thought of John Paul II* (Chicago: Franciscan Herald Press, 1982), p. 50.

address the ambassador of Senegal on 2 December 1978 in these terms:

> Tolerance and peace among the disciples of the great religious confessions are facilitated by the institutions of your country. With regard to these religious confessions, the state keeps the distance which permits the necessary impartiality and the normal distinction between political interests and religious matters. But this distinction is not indifference: the state knows how to mark its esteem for spiritual values and encourage, with justice, the services that religious communities render to the population in the field of education and medical care.

Religious freedom is not, for John Paul II, a matter of mere assertion. Religious freedom requires, and itself creates the conditions for the possibility for, social and political arrangements in which the inviolable rights of the person are respected, a (profoundly anti-totalitarian) distinction between "society" and "state" is constitutionally maintained, and the state thus has limited powers. But, as the pope pointed out in an address to the president of Ghana on 8 May 1980, the church seeks religious freedom not only for the sake of her own evangelical mission but also for the good of society as a whole:

> Since it is the servant of humanity, the Church will always be disposed to collaborate in the promotion of justice, peace, and human dignity by means of the active participation of its members in common initiatives, by proclaiming incessantly that all human beings are created in the image and likeness of God and are, hence, endowed with equal dignity and rights.

In the thought of John Paul II, therefore,

> religious liberty . . . is both an avenue whereby higher motivations can exist in the public order, and a limit [on] politics so that man's higher truth and destiny can be presented and achieved at a depth that is not properly external or political. John Paul has . . . bridged the perplexing question of how religion can be not of this world and yet at the same time be confronted by earthly realities, without destroying the dignity and value of public life and politics. In this he has made a unique contribution

to the history of the idea of freedom by placing it directly in the line of the whole truth about man.[3]

That truth about man includes moral judgments about the right ordering of society. And while it would be unreasonable to expect the pastor of a worldwide church to explicitly endorse democracy as the best available arrangement for the protection of religious freedom and other basic human rights, a brief comment that the pope made while enroute to South America in the spring of 1987 stretches the discussion even further. A reporter on the pope's plane asked the pope whether he would not be meddling in politics during his forthcoming visit to Chile. To this the pope responded, "Yes, yes, I am not the evangelizer of democracy, I am the evangelizer of the Gospel. To the Gospel message, of course, belong all the problems of human rights, and if democracy means human rights it also belongs to the message of the Church."[4]

The sequence within this brief statement is instructive. The church is the church, not a political lobby ("I am the evangelizer of the Gospel"). But the church is neither privatistic nor quietistic ("To the Gospel message, of course, belong all the problems of human rights"). And in the modern world the church has come to understand that the assertion of human rights is insufficient; one has to address the question of institutions of freedom ("And if democracy means human rights it also belongs to the message of the Church"). Religious conviction leads to moral norms, which then lead to issues of the right ordering of social and political institutions. He who says "A," says "B." He who says "religious freedom," in other words, is inevitably involved in saying something about democracy or, at minimum, something about pre-democratic arrangements in which basic human rights are honored and the distinction between society and state is maintained. (The immediate relevance of these concepts to modern political life may be inferred from the pope's direct and indirect role in the creation of *Solidarnosc* in Poland.)

Finally, John Paul II has linked religious freedom or free-

---

3. Ibid., p. 57.
4. John Paul II, quoted in the *New York Times*, 3 Apr. 1987.

dom of conscience to the pursuit of peace in world affairs. In his address to the XXXIV General Assembly of the United Nations on 2 October 1979, he said,

> Man can be wounded in his inner relationship with truth, in his conscience, in his most personal belief, in his view of the world, in his religious faith, and in the sphere of what are known as civil liberties. . . . For centuries the thrust of civilization has been in one direction: that of giving the life of individual political societies a form in which there can be fully safeguarded the objective rights of the spirit, of human conscience and of human creativity, including man's relationship with God.
>
> Besides the acceptance of legal formulas safeguarding the principle of the freedom of the human spirit, such as freedom of thought and expression, religious freedom, and freedom of conscience, structures of social life often exist in which the practical exercise of these freedoms condemns man, in fact if not formally, to become a second-class or third-class citizen, to see compromised his chances of social advancement, his professional career or his access to certain posts of responsibility, and to lose even the possibility of educating his children freely. It is a question of the highest importance that in internal social life, as well as in international life, all human beings in every nation and country should be able to enjoy effectively their full rights under any regime or system.
>
> Only the safeguarding of this real completeness of rights for every human being without discrimination can ensure peace at its very roots.

The religious discussion of religious freedom as the first human right has not been limited to the Roman Catholic Church by any means; in one sense, we can say that the magisterium of the Roman Catholic Church is catching up with Roger Williams. But the doctrine of religious freedom sketched by John Paul II may be of particular interest for several reasons: first, because of the historical transition it bespeaks in Catholic social theory; second, because of the size and impact of the Catholic Church as an international actor; third, because the pope's fundamental argument on behalf of religious freedom is cast not in denominationally specific terms but in concepts and language accessible to all people of goodwill, irrespective of their religious convictions or lack thereof; and fourth, because of the pope's linkage between religious freedom and certain political-institutional arrangements, and between religious freedom and peace. Thus the theory of religious freedom adumbrated by John Paul II is of special significance in natively pluralistic societies like the United States, as well as, of course, in our luxuriantly plural world.

IV. THE TEMPTATIONS OF RELIGIOUS FREEDOM

In a legendary lecture he gave to a generation of American Jesuits during pre-ordination retreats, John Courtney Murray used to warn against the "temptations of the vows." The vow of obedience could be a temptation to intellectual sloth. The vow of chastity could be a temptation to aridity in human relationships. The vow of poverty could be a temptation to irresponsibility in the use of material goods. Beware, Murray warned, the temptations of the vows. The good of the vows can be corrupted if one is not aware of the moral failings that one would like to "excuse" on the grounds of one's commitment to those vows.

In an analogical way, the good of religious freedom involves social and political temptations that ought to be resisted.

In a situation like that of the United States, for example, we can too blithely assume that the institutionalization of religious freedom has solved all those knotty problems involved in the relationship between moral norms and social structures or public policy.

If the "right of religious freedom" is reduced to an ensemble of constitutional and legal procedures—if, that is, we ignore the "public" meaning of religious freedom out of a self-satisfied complacency over the legal protections afforded the "private" meaning of this right—then we have traduced the right of religious freedom in its fullest meaning. Put another way, if the right of religious freedom is reduced in public understanding to a matter of individual "taste" such that the moral norms attendant on religious truth claims are deemed merely matters of "preference" in our public discourse, we will soon find ourselves (as we may indeed have already found ourselves) in a situation in which public moral discourse ceases, and public moral emoting is the order of the day. The situation described by Alasdair MacIntyre in the early chapters of *After*

Virtue comes immediately to mind here: we can no longer say "You *ought* to . . ." in public life. And if, as I suggested previously, democratic governance is a never-finished experiment testing human capacities for self-rule, the reduction of the right of religious freedom to its "interior" meaning alone, fundamental as that meaning is, can yield a situation in which our society becomes, in Stanley Hauerwas's terms, "morally and spiritually empty at its core." The public role of religion is, as the analysis in Part II of this essay makes clear, a core ingredient in the perdurance of the democratic experiment. Ignoring this social fact is one temptation of religious freedom.

There is also an ecclesiological temptation involved in the right of religious freedom. How shall we think of a situation like that of the Roman Catholic Church in Poland prior to 1989, in which the church was reasonably free to pursue its evangelical and pastoral mission but was also the primary institutional opposition to the social and political claims of the state? On the one hand, one ought to be grateful that such an institutional opposition existed. On the other hand, the fact of that institutional opposition may have been a temptation for the Catholic Church—a temptation to ignore or minimize the necessity for other, specifically political institutions of opposition. Did the Catholic Church in Poland run the risk of becoming over time a kind of domesticated opposition, while other opposition forces such as *Solidarnosc* were allowed to wither? Similar temptations faced the church in the Philippines in the wake of the insurrection that led to the fall of Ferdinand Marcos.

Taken seriously, the "public" meaning of the right of religious freedom or freedom of conscience requires a commitment on the part of the religious community to help facilitate the creation of (or to strengthen, where they exist) those myriad other social institutions which comprise that "society" which is prior to the state, and whose health and well-being are essential to democratic governance. As the preceding analysis shows, the human rights concerns of the religious community—even in terms of the right of religious freedom or freedom of conscience—are not fully met when that community's functioning is legally protected.

Finally, there is what we might call a "doctrinal" temptation in the right of religious freedom. Religious belief involves truth claims about matters of ultimate consequence. The "procedures" of religious freedom as worked out in a denominational society like the United States can create what might appear to be virtually irresistible cultural pressures toward taking the edge off religious truth claims, as they are understood by the sundry religious communities of the country. John Murray Cuddihy's analysis of this phenomenon in *No Offense: Civil Religion and Protestant Taste*[5] may be taken as a curmudgeonly, recent exploration of the problem. Does the right of religious freedom *necessarily* yield a "civil religion of civility" in which religious truth claims are not seriously engaged but muted (and, ultimately, dissolved) out of a concern for showing "good taste"? Is the net result of all this a least common denominator, religion-of-the-American-way-of-life? So Cuddihy argues (echoing Will Herberg a generation before), and Stanley Hauerwas (in his essay entitled "Freedom of Religion: A Subtle Temptation"[6]) is inclined to agree, although he would most probably reject the qualifier "necessarily."

On the other side of the debate, Richard Neuhaus and many others have argued that it is precisely the kinds of social and political arrangements we enjoy in the United States that create the conditions for the possibility of engaging religious differences forthrightly—in both their internal-doctrinal and their public-policy respects—within the bond of a democratic civility that eventually sharpens theological understandings. Neuhaus and those on his side of the debate would recognize the temptation that Cuddihy analyzes and Hauerwas warns against, but they would see it as precisely that, a temptation, and not a necessary consequence of the right and practice of religious freedom.

That debate, like many of the other debates referred to in this essay, seems likely to continue. That it will is perhaps itself a compliment to both the "interior" and the "public" meanings of the right of religious freedom.

---

5. Cuddihy, *No Offense: Civil Religion and Protestant Taste* (New York: Seabury Press, 1978).

6. Hauerwas, "Freedom of Religion: A Subtle Temptation," *Soundings* 72 (Summer/Fall 1989): 317-40.

The Story of an Encounter

Paul T. Stallsworth

The intriguing title of this meeting, "The Structure of Freedom: Correlations, Causes, and Cautions," surely played a large part in attracting the twenty-eight conferees to the conference table in the Grant Room of New York's Union League Club. After words of welcome and introduction, Pastor Richard John Neuhaus, moderator of the conference, outlined the direction of the two-day discussion. The conference, said Neuhaus, would proceed in this manner: Peter Berger would address the alleged correlation of liberties, Raymond Gastil would outline the conflicted nature of the freedoms, George Weigel would attempt to establish that religious freedom is the first human right, and Mary Ann Glendon would add a note of caution on the understanding of freedom in American law.

CORRELATIONS OR SERENDIPITIES?

Dr. Peter L. Berger, the Director of the Institute for the Study of Economic Culture and a professor at Boston University, opened the conference by summarizing his essay. "Basically what I am concerned with in my essay are the empirical relationships between a number of institutional processes in the modern world; then I draw some evaluative implications from those relationships. I should emphasize that what I am interested in in this essay is the relationship between *institutions* and *institutional*

56

processes, not the relationship between ideas. In the humanities there tends to be the general notion that institutions embody ideas, which to some extent, of course, is true. For example, the institutions of democracy do embody, however imperfectly, democratic ideas. But I think that most of the time the assumption is false or at least considerably misleading, because institutions are patterned human activity which involves interests as much as ideas. Also, this patterned human activity is really no more than habit, the reasons for which may long have been forgotten. So in my essay I am not concerned with the ways in which the idea of liberty can be argued; I am concerned with the institutional processes that in one way or another relate to the aims of liberty."

Then Berger noted what he deemed to be the two key relationships—the relationship between liberalism and democracy, and the relationship between democracy and capitalism. According to Berger, "Both relationships embody ideas and ideals of various sorts, but they also relate to very concrete and empirically accessible institutions."

Berger touched on liberal democracy first: "We use the term 'liberal democracy,' which assumes that there is such a thing as illiberal democracy. I find this very important to emphasize, particularly in our present climate of opinion, where there has been a resurgence, in America and to some extent in Europe, of emphasizing democracy and the democratic idea."

Berger then took on the second key relationship— democracy and capitalism. "There the serendipity becomes most interesting. There is nothing in the notion of democracy which says that democracy must be linked to a capitalist economy. In other words, there is nothing logically contradictory about the ideal of democratic socialism. Nor is it impossible for capitalist economies, as we empirically know them, to be linked to authoritarian regimes of one sort or another. The linkage, again, is not in the realm of ideas; the linkage is in the realm of empirical, institutional, social realities. As I read the evidence, one can express the relationship between these two kinds of institutions rather simply, and a number of people have said this: Capitalism is a necessary but not sufficient condition for democracy. Capitalism is clearly not sufficient, since other variables must intervene. There have been in the past and there are today nondemocratic, capitalist societies. But so far, all existing democracies of the world have capitalist economies and are indeed linked to the international capitalist system.

"Why should this be so? Is there some strange mystery? I don't think so. It has to do with the way in which these institutions function in the modern situation. Under modern conditions there are only two basic mechanisms for human economic organizations. One is the mechanism of the market, and the other is the political mechanism, the political system of decision-making. These two mechanisms never exist in pure form. We know that. There is always a mix between the two. Even Hong Kong is not a laissez-faire paradise, and even the Soviet Union in its more rigid days had an underground capitalist economy. But it makes sense to say that Hong Kong is capitalist and the Soviet Union was not. There are no third ways. There are only various combinations of these two mechanisms, with one or the other holding the dominant role. So, if we are talking about alternatives to capitalism in the modern world, we are talking about various forms of socialism. Everything else, I think, is rhetoric and illusion.

"Why would a democratic regime be more closely linked to a capitalist rather than a socialist way of organizing the economy? While the argument can be enormously complex, fundamentally the issue is quite simple: socialism empirically means a quantum leap in the power of the state in actually taking over the production machinery of a society. The modern state is already enormously powerful, even without that. Because of the means of coercion and control available to the modern state, a little Swiss canton has more power than the Roman Empire had over its citizens. Now, when you add to this already enormous power the power to run the economy, the power to make basic decisions about production and distribution, democracy, which is essentially the limitation of state power, becomes all the more difficult. Again, I'm not saying it becomes impossible. But it becomes very improbable indeed.

"Therefore, it is not at all surprising that there is not today and has not been in the past a single case of a democratic socialist society. And I wouldn't hold my breath waiting for one, because I think the chances are against it. And please don't mention Sweden. Sweden isn't a socialist society. It's a capitalist society with a capitalist economy with a very well-developed welfare state."

Berger completed his summary by relating his comments to religious liberty and to religion. "We can subsume religious freedom among other freedoms. For example, in the American political and constitutional tradition, freedom of religion is linked to freedom of speech, freedom of assembly, and so on. If we make these linkages, the correlations hold; they are relevant. That is, if we are concerned with religious freedom, we should opt for democracy; and if we are concerned with democracy, we should opt for capitalism. Democratic capitalism is again, empirically, the best guarantor of religious freedom. I think the facts bear me out on that.

"But there is another dimension that in the final analysis is perhaps more interesting. Here I go a little bit beyond discussing empirical evidence of one sort or another. I think that religious freedom is more than one freedom on a list of liberties that we would want guaranteed. In a very real sense it is the one freedom that underlies all of the others. I'm not saying this as a Christian or a theologian or a religious believer. It's difficult to put oneself in a different skin, but I think I would say the same thing if I were an atheist. Why am I saying this? Because I think religion emphasizes, by its very existence, the finitude and relativity of all human institutions. Religion, at its core, intends transcendence. It puts the human condition, with its history and its social arrangements, into a different frame of reference. This relativizes everything human. I'm convinced that religion is concerned at its very center with things of another world, and the affairs of this world are thereby relativized. That has never sat well with despots. A tyrant almost always has an enormously important sense of himself and of his own power; he doesn't welcome reminders of finitude and mortality. That has always been the case. That's why modern tyrannies, totalitarian states, always want to control religious institutions more than others. This is so not because religion is particularly dangerous in an obvious political way, but because by its very existence religion challenges the omnipotence of the state.

"If I'm right about this, there is a final paradox to consider. The role I've just sketched can be described as a worldly function of religion. It is a secular service of religion. This is a service that the church or religious institutions of whatever nature render to the world. Fine. But the church can do that only as long as it remains otherworldly. As soon as it becomes secularized, as soon as its agenda becomes a worldly agenda, it can no longer serve that purpose. It loses this utility to society. This is a paradox in ideas, but it is not at all a paradox in the way institutions function. As soon as you perceive it, it becomes almost self-evident: if the church is totally engaged in an agenda that by definition is finite, it can no longer remind the tyrant of the finitude of all human affairs. In order to serve the world, religion has to remain otherworldly."

Jim Finn of Freedom House was the first challenger. He had a problem with Berger's use of the word "serendipity." " 'Serendipity' is a nice little word of fairly recent coinage in the English language. What it really means is the ability, or the gift, to discover without effort and without intention something wonderful and useful. Serendipity is the kind of thing President Reagan seemed to have in the early years of his administration and later seemed to lose. Although it's a gift that some people have, it's not a gift that they will necessarily have forever. But that doesn't seem to be the operative meaning of the word in Professor Berger's essay. Maybe the way Peter uses the word is the way people customarily use it. Or perhaps it can be twisted in that direction."

Berger, unwilling to engage in a semantic joust, replied, "I defer to you utterly, totally, and humbly on matters of the English language. All I meant by 'serendipitous' is that you look for one thing and you find another. So I surrender. Scratch the word 'serendipity.' "

Categorical Problems

Dr. Joshua Muravchik of American Enterprise Institute was the second challenger. "For all of his emphasis on empiricism," contended Muravchik, "Professor Berger left 'illiberal democracy' an abstraction. He didn't offer any examples in his essay or in his oral presentation. So I suspect that the concept is questionable."

Berger was ready with a reply: "Historically, all of the democracies were at one time illiberal. You should look at England in the early nineteenth century. Take the trouble to look at that system from below to find out what it meant for a working-class individual who didn't have the franchise and who had a horrendous, coercive apparatus sitting on top of him. The English common law around the turn of the century— 1800 or so—was horrible!"

"But why should we call that democracy?" Neuhaus asked.

Berger answered, "Because it had the basic democratic mechanisms already in place—for example, elections. All you could say against it was that the franchise was rather limited. But that brings you to the interesting question in democratic theory: How large does the franchise have to be before you call it a democracy? So it's useful to keep in mind that liberalism and democracy aren't the same. We may well find cases like that of nineteenth-century England again, even if today, fortunately, it's difficult to think of one."

Professor Joachim Maitre, Dean of the College of Communication at Boston University, did not like Berger's dabbling with Marxist ideas. Maitre explained why autobiographically: "I grew up in East Germany. As a fourteen-year-old, together with two classmates, I was tried by an official court of a German youth organization for having challenged the very definition of socialism—from each according to his ability, to each according to his need. This definition, of course, indicates the massive power of the state to tax and redistribute. After the trial, which resulted in our being sent to a labor camp for about four weeks, a history professor took me aside and said, 'Shut up, even though you're right.' This man wore the badge of the Party, so we realized very quickly that the mark of socialism in action is hypocrisy. The point was and is that if you play by the rules, you will have a fairly comfortable life.

"Now, you speak of the distributive power of the state, Peter. That's a Marxist term. Taxation is the issue here. You may allow free production, but then you come in and allow the state to siphon off what you consider a just amount. The mere term 'redistribution of income,' which has become so accepted in Western society, contradicts capitalism."

"No, I don't think so," said Berger.

Maitre continued his line of questioning: "Then what exactly is capitalism? How are you going to define it?"

Berger offered a standard definition: "Capitalism is a 'mode of production,' that being a Marxian term. It is characterized by two elements that every good definition of capitalism must contain. One is that market forces play a very important role in economic decisions. That is, it is market decision-making over political decision-making. The second is that the basic means of production are privately owned."

Maitre, still not satisfied, asked, "But exactly where is there capitalism? Where is there the free expression of economic sovereignty, the incentive motive that can be killed off entirely by the redistributive power of the state?"

"The incentive motive can be killed, but it isn't," Berger came back.

"But it is. It is," Maitre protested.

Then it was Berger's turn to protest: "I would dispute that. Look, from the viewpoint of an Ayn Randian ideal, there is no capitalism in the world. Not even in Hong Kong, which is ruled by a strange conspiracy of British civil servants and Chinese millionaires. I am not for a moment disputing that there are mixed cases. In fact, my whole argument is that there are mixed cases. But I don't think we know empirically the exact point at which the economic mechanism tilts the political implications in one direction or the other. To put it more precisely, I can't tell you what degree of socialism is compatible with democracy, or what degree of capitalism is compatible with nondemocratic governance.

"We aren't sure what happens with marketization. At our institute at Boston University, we now have a project looking at cases like China. How much marketization is possible before the political system is subject to change? Or you can ask the opposite question: To what extent can socialism be modified without endangering the monopoly of power of the Communist Party? The conservative communists in China and elsewhere are right in worrying about this."

Moderator Neuhaus then moved in to moderate: "Peter, you do stipulate in your essay that there are no pure types."

"There *are* no pure types!" exclaimed Berger. "But to say that there is no difference between the way the economies used to be organized in eastern Europe and the way they are organized in western Europe, to say that they are all forms of socialism, isn't very useful. The empirical reality—economically, socially, and politically—between those countries commonly called capitalist and those countries commonly called socialist is glaring."

Philosopher Frithjof Bergmann of the University of Michigan was the next to question Berger. "Even though Professor Berger claims that much of his approach is very empirical, at some critical points his discussion becomes very abstract. For example, the proposition that you can't have democracy without capitalism depends upon a great deal of abstraction. It would come out very, very differently if instead of making this proposition he would say, 'Well, we have mixed types in practice and all over the place, and there are many socialist countries that to a considerable degree are democratic.'"

"But I'm not prepared to say that," responded Berger. "All my inclinations as a bourgeois Viennese are to concede your point. But I can't do that, because I think you're mistaken. The only abstract thing here is how we conceptualize, and this is inevitable."

Bergmann replied, "I want to claim that there are all sorts of combinations of democracy and socialism that are possible, and that it's very possible to have democracy with economic systems that are partly capitalist and partly socialist." On that point Bergmann and Berger respectfully agreed to disagree.

Ideas and Institutions

Dr. Liah Greenfeld of Harvard worried about Berger's apparent de-emphasis on the role of ideas in the historical emergence of democracy. She began with this comment: "Professor

Berger tries to explain the empirical connection betweeen liberalism and democracy. He equates modernization with the evolution of the great means and equipment of the modern state and the disappearance or weakening of traditions that restrict the state. Democracy, then, becomes the functional equivalent of such restricting traditions. It emerges because the state becomes so strong, and there are no other means to restrict its strength. If this is so, then history is indeed the march of freedom on earth. According to Berger's logic, it is precisely the strength of the socialist state that brings about the need for democracy, because in a socialist state the need for restriction of state power is so strong."

"There might be a need for democracy," broke in Neuhaus, "but why should it come about if it is against the interests of the socialist state?"

Berger followed by noting that "if democracy arose because the modern state is so powerful, it will arise even more under socialism. Maybe so. But democracy's chance of realization is much smaller under socialism. As long as you have a socialist state in place as a functioning reality, the chances of establishing democratic controls aren't very good." (Berger's comment clearly did not enjoy the experience of what is called the Revolution of 1989.)

Greenfeld didn't answer the Neuhaus-Berger challenge, but she did go on to give some reasons, which were quite unrelated to Berger's notions of serendipity, for the rise of liberal democracy. "My explanation has to do with the logic of ideas. I can describe it here very simply. It goes back to a certain revolution in religion. It starts in the increased emphasis on what was interpreted as a religious truth at a certain point in religious history. It starts with the English Reformation. In the very beginning of this period, man is defined as a rational being, and this becomes the most important assumption in religious, political, and social history for several centuries. Since man is defined as a rational being, since man is seen as being created in the image of his Creator, since man in his rationality is most similar to the Creator, man deserves respect. This becomes the reason for respecting any man. This is the reason for liberalism—that is, respect for the liberties and rights of the individual. What then emerges is the liberty of the individual conscience. From the same proposition—man is a rational being—emerges another value. And that is the value of equality. Because man is essentially a rational being, any man is equal to any other man. Since there is this essential equality, every man can decide for himself, and every man has the right to participate in collective decisions, in political decisions. This is the basis of democracy. Democracy is the institutionalization of this value." The ideas behind liberal democracy, Greenfeld concluded, were the content of sixteenth-century English idealism and nationalism.

Neuhaus reinforced Greenfeld's statement: "The whole argument of A. D. Lindsay and others is that the history of ideas undergirds democracy. That is distinct from Berger's proposal. Still, I'm sympathetic to Lindsay's argument. Berger seems to be shortchanging the history of ideas and its impact on democratic developments."

In response, Berger defended his more sociological position: "Historically, if you look at Europe, the rise of democracy coincided with and was related to the development of modern capitalism as an economic system. The bourgeoisie was the class that was the carrier of capitalism and democracy. So, this is not a mystery.

"Am I shortchanging the history of ideas? I hope not. I'm not a materialist. I do believe that ideas play a role in history, but their efficacy is always limited. It almost never happens that ideas are realized, period. Ideas are usually realized through a series of institutional refractions where very frequently what comes out in the end is something very different from what the initiators of those processes intended."

Not ready for this topic to fade away, Dr. Richard Hutcheson, an author, spoke on behalf of the importance of ideas. "Professor Berger's discussion of religious freedom at least points to the theoretical framework that is especially necessary in understanding the relationship of the kinds of freedom in the American experience. He gives a fine exposition of the heart of the political theology of Roger Williams. The coming together in the American experience of the Puritan tradition, the Enlightenment, and religious pluralism created a very special experiment. These ideas have been highly significant players, not only in the past but also in recent history. You can point to them in Carter's human-rights emphasis and in much of what Reagan said about worldwide liberty."

Threats to Religion?

Phyllis Zagano, a New York–based journalist now at Boston University's College of Communication, moved on to another line of inquiry by describing an irony of religious freedom. "Religious freedom, of course, involves the freedom not to believe. So it appears that the religious freedom that is caused or guaranteed or created or protected by democracy includes the freedom not to believe. The question then becomes this: Can religious freedom actually cause the removal of religion from the public sector? I speak specifically about 'secular humanism' as a kind of burgeoning religious belief in America and about a kind of religious socialism. Those are two kinds of threats. Therefore, the democratic capitalism that protects religious freedom is protecting religion's ability to be destroyed."

"That indeed is a risk," Berger agreed. Then to Zagano's irony he added a paradox. "Religion relativizes, because the religious frame of reference makes all human actions in the end look absurdly insignificant. That is a worldly service. The seriousness of the worldly order, in terms of religion, is a joke. And as I've said, tyrants do not like to be joked about. Religion can perform this function, which is a worldly function, only if it is outside that worldly frame of reference."

In response to Berger, Andrew Sullivan, who writes for *The New Republic,* assumed the role of questioner. "How can you say that? What religion? How? In one statement you tried to say so much. Do you distinguish between Augustinian views of the worldly order and Thomistic views? Both of them do not say, in the same way, that all worldly functions are absurdly insignificant. And to use the word 'religion' in such a sweeping way is not very respectful toward the different arguments within different religions."

Unruffled, Berger answered, "Let me be even more reckless than you accuse me of being. I would include non-Christian religions. I would include Buddhism. I would include Hinduism. Of course I'm saying a lot in a few sentences, but what else can you do in an essay? I promise you that for the rest of today and tonight I could give a lecture amplifying my point.

"I think at the core of religion is the experience of transcendence. That is the defining, characteristic aspect of religious experience and religious thought. What does transcendence mean? It means that the human condition is an antechamber; it is not the ultimate reality."

Neuhaus broke in to suggest a qualifier: "But transcendence does not exclude a theologically legitimated sense of urgency about the tasks of history."

"Of course not," Berger emphatically stated. "But the tasks of history are put in a frame of reference that transcends history. They are not ultimate. This is true in Augustine, Thomas, and even Confucius, who is usually cited as being a very secular thinker rather than a religious one."

Somewhat later in the discussion, someone asked whether democratic capitalism works like an acid on religion. To this, Berger replied, "It is very important to distinguish between capitalism as a particular economic arrangement and modernity in general, which need not take capitalist forms. I have argued that modernization does indeed contain intrinsic forces that are at least in tension with religion. This has to do with the role of science and technology and with pluralism. It has nothing to do with capitalism. It is, after all, the same under socialist conditions. Yes, in democratic capitalist societies, religion faces certain threats, but those mainly have to do with modernity and not with capitalism. While democratic capitalism suffers the same pangs of modernization as any other form of society in the modern world, it nevertheless provides better institutional protections for the religious individual and the religious institution."

Agreeing with Berger on the relationship between capitalism and modernity, Father Francis Canavan of Fordham offered an aside. "It's true that capitalism and modernity are linked, just as socialism and modernity are linked. I would suggest a very unusual way of disentangling these relationships. The only good thing that the Iranian revolution has done is that it has opened up this perspective for us: from the viewpoint of an Iranian mullah, capitalism and socialism are the twin satans of modernity. The mullah is right. From his viewpoint capitalism and socialism emerge from one phenomenon."

Sullivan was still unconvinced by Berger's argument and said so. "But the philosophical basis of capitalism may be antithetic to certain parts of religion. For example, the very understanding of man and political structures being radically based on the state of nature has profound social consequences for the way we think about ourselves. That is antithetic to certain, though not all, forms of religion.

"The religious individual is a human being and of course has a body. Therefore, he or she can be attacked. The question is whether his or her conscience can be attacked. He or she, in the last resort, can be and has been burned or imprisoned or murdered or tortured. But, to be specific, Christianity's teachings imply that that is not that important and that there is a radical understanding of freedom of conscience that is so scornful of political structures that they become completely irrelevant."

Berger replied, "The notion that only the body can be harmed by society and that the mind cannot be is wrong. The mind can be affected by society even more than the body can. The social pressures, political or otherwise, on the conscience are enormous. So it's not simply a question of protecting people from being burned at the stake. It's a question of allowing social space in which a particular kind of conscience can be formed and institutionalized."

"I agree," Sullivan responded. "If democratic capitalism, based upon certain understandings of material self-preservation of the individual and property rights and so on, inculcates certain views within society about the priority of this world over the next and the priority of individuals over religious institutions, then you are in a situation where the very structure that allegedly allows 'space' becomes insidiously anti-religious."

Neuhaus then commented on Sullivan's comment: "In other words, democratic capitalism robs religion of its public potency. Democratic capitalism tends to put religion in the marketplace, like any consumer item. Therefore, religion is

robbed of what it presumably can do—namely, to make publicly potent truth claims. In that sense, democratic capitalism,
under the guise of being a friend of religion, becomes an enemy
of authentic religion. And then religion isn't able to play the
role in society that it can and should play."

Berger noted, "There have been several philosophical
bases of capitalism. Certainly in northern Europe, western
Europe, and North America, capitalism through most of its
history developed in strongly religious cultures, Protestant cultures, which did not have any of these implications."

Rabbi David Novak, who teaches at the University of
Virginia, pointed out that the most basic threat to religion is
neither freedom nor democratic capitalism—it is the very language of religion. "Religion entails, like any other human en-
deavor, the transmission of a specific language. The fact is that
unless the institutions of society enable a religious language to
be cultivated, it will not have the structure for the formation of
religious conscience. For example, studies examining the
degeneration of the German language under Nazi totalitarianism show that language can be changed to such an extent
that what I consider to be the principles of my conscience can
become unintelligible to others in society."

Stephen Post of the Center for Biomedical Ethics, Case
Western Reserve University, was a bit uncomfortable with
Berger's emphasis on the otherworldly character of religion.
Said Post, "Professor Berger is right to say that religion must
maintain its otherworldly character in order to make worldly
authority penultimate. My only fear is that in overstressing the
indirect political implications of religion we might forget about
religion's social-activist mode. When we assign religion the
minimalist function of maintaining a sphere of inviolable conscience, we might also need to suggest that religion will always
have reformist inclinations, especially in its Protestant versions.
Sometimes these will verge on the secular, and they will appear
worldly. But their orientation, their impulse, their passion is
nevertheless theological."

Echoing Post's concerns was Stephen Bates, an author
from Cambridge, Massachusetts. "Religion as religion may
have something distinctive to offer in the social and political

marketplace. After all, religion is the only institutional speaker bringing transcendent values as a complex to real-world issues and questions. So I'm not sure it's right to say that religion becomes just another interest group when it becomes a public actor. There might be trade-offs involved, so that we might consider it worthwhile for religion to lose some of its other-worldliness if it has something unique to say to worldly issues."

Berger then clarified his position. "Not for a moment was I suggesting a program of religious quietism and withdrawal from the world as the only possible public stance of religion. That's totally against everything I have ever thought as a Christian. That's not the point. The point is simply that when a religious institution regards a political agenda, or any other this-worldly agenda, as the essence of what it does, at that point it loses its transcendent character. Discerning the point at which a religious institution takes on a this-worldly agenda isn't all that difficult. I don't find it difficult to discern in listening to religious people talk about their commitments."

Capitalism, Democracy, and Socialism

Several of the participants pondered the alleged conditions and preconditions of democracy. Berger led the way: "In countries with amazingly different cultures and religious traditions, once the possibility of democracy emerges, most people like it. I find that very impressive. The argument that Judeo-Christian values or Western traditions or something of the sort are a precondition for democracy is difficult to sustain. The most important cases which weaken that argument are India and Japan. In both cases there are no dominant Western traditions. These societies are not Western at all in terms of values."

Dean Curry of Messiah College pushed Berger a bit. "Sidney Hook argues powerfully that humanism, even secular humanism, can form a viable basis for the democratic experiment. Would you go so far as to agree with Sidney Hook that humanism is sufficient?"

"I don't agree with Sidney Hook, but I don't disagree with him either," Berger replied.

Neuhaus then observed, "You're always so wishy-washy, Peter."

Earlier Berger had claimed that capitalism is a necessary but not sufficient condition of democracy. Now Francis Canavan asked why this is so. Berger answered with an anecdote. "Let me tell you a story. It was an 'aha' experience for me, and it happened quite a few years ago in Tanzania, which had then and has now essentially a socialist economy, although, like many of these countries, it's trying to backtrack. At a party I overheard a conversation between a dean from a local university and the editor of the only English-language newspaper, which was then a party newspaper. The issue was that a young man who worked for the university wanted to work for the newspaper—he wanted to change jobs. This editor was trying to convince the dean to let him do that. I wanted to understand what they were talking about, so they explained the whole thing to me. It was an interesting progression of explanations. They began by telling me that this guy had been given a government scholarship to the university, and in exchange for that he had to perform five years of work in a government or para-state or party organization. That's fair enough. It's like people getting federal grants and having to work for the federal government in return. Under that provision, the guy had to ask permission to change jobs. Still, that's fair enough. But then it became perfectly clear that any desirable job in Tanzania was governmentally controlled. The only vocational space in which this individual could escape government control was the space of a street-corner vendor.

"That's the answer to your question. If all the major productive machineries of a society are under political control, there are very few places of refuge, because every desirable means of livelihood is under political control. Capitalism, on the other hand, provides social space in which people can make a living without being directly dependent on political controls."

Berger also illustrated his point by describing Singapore. "It's a society that any sociologist should be interested in. It's a totally artificial society. Everything is artificial—from the architecture to the language. In Singapore it's very clear what ownership means. It means what ownership means in any authoritarian society: if you really oppose the government, the government will hurt you, and that includes your rights of ownership. That's what authoritarianism means. If the government doesn't like you, it will take away your license, it will look at your tax returns for the last fifty years, and it will be able to destroy you. But if you don't oppose the government—and 97 percent of the people of Singapore don't—you operate with what we regard as normal ownership rights."

Nina Shea of the Puebla Institute then mentioned a most unexpected precondition of democracy. "I disagree with the proposition that technology has made modern state control more effective. Granted, technology has made more centralized state power possible. But, in fact, modern technology has also made democracy possible and in a sense is a pre-condition for democracy. Computers and copy machines and roads and cars and maps and education and air travel can actually be threats to totalitarian control."

The Churches and the Liberties

Dr. James Nuechterlein, formerly of *The Cresset* and Valparaiso University, was concerned that today's American churches are not more concerned about freedom—religious, political, and economic—in the world. He conjectured that some of the ecclesiastical powers that be have taken over, or have been taken over by, a Marxist idea of alienation. This is evidenced in the strongholds of liberation theology in American Protestantism and American Catholicism. Unfortunately, he said, "that kind of Christianity loses its power to act as a check on the power of the state. This is especially true if it has bought into the revolutionary myth. Because if it has bought into that myth, it has bought into the power of the state—since revolutions in power inevitably involve the state. A Christianity that has bought into the revolutionary myth is no longer a check on the power of the state; it is a reinforcement of the state."

Adding more substance to Nuechterlein's claim was Dr. Kent Hill, Executive Director of the Institute on Religion and Democracy. "The basic thesis of the morning is this: There's a very interesting coincidence between regimes that allow a certain amount of economic freedom and certain kinds of political liberty and religious liberty. In fact, the thesis claims that capitalism is a necessary but not sufficient condition for democracy. That line of analysis has not been substantially challenged here this morning. Most people here find that idea acceptable, though we quibble over how it's argued and defined and so on. But the basic thesis doesn't seem to be in dispute.

"However, outside the confines of this room this thesis is in great dispute. In the circles in which I move—in the church and seminary worlds—the proposition that is much more common goes like this: The more Christian one is, the more committed to the gospel one is, the more naturally antagonistic to capitalism and the more inclined toward socialism one will be. To be sure, the kind of socialisms that have thus far emerged are not the assumed ideal. But as near as I can tell, that thesis, which is mainly a faith claim, is pretty much impervious to empirical examination. You can argue until you're blue in the face about which systems help poor people more, and still you'll find an incredibly thick stone wall that obstructs challenges to this dominant set of propositions. It takes a lot more than having good empirical evidence to break through that. Chesterton said that to cure an insane person you don't need a logician, you need an exorcist. At some point I'm afraid that's what we need to break through this wall."

"In certain religious circles in the West there's a curious bias toward the socialist vision," Berger agreed. Then, agreeing with Hill, he concluded the first session of the conference with these comments: "It's striking how absolutely impermeable this religious mind-set is to evidence. There's always a good socialism around the corner. It was in Chile, but then it was squelched. Then it was the Prague spring. Or then, incredibly, it was in Mozambique.

"What can one do about this? It has to do with capitalism and democracy being such prosaic, pragmatic things compared with the mythopoetic vision of socialism. But I don't know what one can do. I'm not an exorcist; I'm a social scientist. There's only one absolutely, empirically proven recipe for the people you describe, and that is protracted residence in a socialist society. The Kissinger Commission made a crazy proposal to bring ten thousand Central American students to the United States; unfortunately, they would all go home socialist. What we should do is send ten thousand Central American students to the Soviet Union at the expense of the U.S. government. We know what happens to people who study at Soviet universities: for the rest of their lives they're impervious to Soviet propaganda and to the socialist dream.

"I'm often reminded of a statement that has been ascribed to Sigmund Freud, though I could never find the reference: 'The voice of reason is quiet but persistent.' Although I've made it quite clear that I don't believe that history is the march of reason on earth or that ideas dominate history, there is something to reason. The slow, patient, undogmatic accumulation of evidence does, in the end, have an effect. That is all I know to say. I'm not a preacher; I don't know how to convert these people. But they have to be confronted, again and again, with the real world. I think the pressure of evidence does have an effect. And in terms of the socialist intelligentsia in various Western countries, there have been some interesting changes. The situation today is obviously not what it was in the early 1970s. The most dramatic example of this is France. And in other Western countries there has been a change in intellectual climate that is at least partially due to the accumulation and communication of evidence."

FREEDOMS IN CONFLICT?

As the second presenter of the first day of the conference, Raymond Gastil, an author who was formerly at Freedom House, introduced his essay. Before getting to the bad news of freedoms in conflict, he spoke about the good news of the birth of the freedoms. "We're considering political rights or freedoms on the one hand, and economic and religious freedoms on the other. All three kinds of freedom, it seems to me, developed together in Western civilization. They developed together as part of the general breakdown of the hierarchical society, and they have progressed together for at least the last two hundred years. They're very closely related to the development of modernity.

"I believe there is a causative relationship between the three kinds of freedom. There may be a certain causative relationship in a social-scientific sense, but in fact all we have is the historical record. This record shows that the freedoms matured together and that together they diffused from the developed parts of the world to the less developed parts of the world. Admittedly, we have no independent cases that could be used to verify any necessary causative relationships among the three kinds of freedom. The best predictor of democracy is probably the extent and intensity of a particular country's relationship with Western countries in which democracy flourishes. Somebody pointed out to me that if you look at the British Empire and if you ask which of the countries are democratic at the end of the empire, you'll find that the answer is closely correlated with the number of years that those countries were in the empire.

"We have the case known as the welfare state. Peter Berger doesn't want me to talk about it, but this case is of some significance. Some of the welfare states—like the United Kingdom, for example—are a good ways down the road of nationalization. After all, it nationalized the profession of medicine, many of the heavy industries, and so on. The interesting thing about these efforts is that although they didn't go all the way, there is little evidence that the way they did go really had much of an effect on political and religious freedoms. This suggests that the connection between the three kinds of freedom is rather loose."

The loose connection between the freedoms, according to Gastil, can be spotted "as closed societies open up. When they do, they become more democratic politically, more market oriented, and more tolerant of religious differences. Those three will go together. I see that happening because of the force of cultural diffusion and the necessity of joining a world that is already characterized by the three different kinds of freedom."

Then came Gastil's bad, or cautionary, news—which is the tension between types of freedoms. "The most critical trade-off in freedoms is the conflict between individual freedoms and collective freedoms. In this regard I tell my favorite story about a little island on which there are ten people. Six of them want to build a boat to get off the island; four want to build an airplane. But unless all ten support one project or the other, neither project will prove successful. The six win by majority vote, which means that the four may well feel that they are victims of a majoritarian tyranny."

Liah Greenfeld was not persuaded by Gastil's point about the diffusion of liberties. "After all," she said, "there are some countries which came in contact with the West that didn't immediately accept the ideas of freedom. The example closest to my mind, if not to my heart, is Russia and the Soviet Union. Growing up in that country was both a privilege and a misfortune. It came in contact with the West very early—in fact, in the seventeenth century. Since then Russia has been (until recently) systematically resistant to the advance of liberty, though it did borrow many ideas from the West.

"Ideas by themselves," Greenfeld concluded, "do not determine development in society. Objective social forces by themselves do not determine development. What does determine development is the establishment of systems of interest. These systems include national volition, hate, sympathy, and identity, all of which came into being when the nation-state came into being."

Making a similar statement was Joshua Muravchik. "As we examine the empirical correlation between democracy and capitalism," he noted, "we assume that it just happened, without paying adequate attention to the human wills that made it happen. There is nothing to be learned from defining Nazism as capitalism or socialism. Nazism was a specific product of the will and ideas of Adolf Hitler and some of his colleagues. American democracy and capitalism are, most importantly, the products of the ideas and deliberate planning of Thomas Jefferson and some of his associates. Socialism and the earlier dictatorship of the communist kind in the Soviet Union are products of the specific plans of Lenin and his associates. This contradicts Berger's claim in his essay that results usually contradict intentions: in each of these cases, the systems and the resulting political economies were precisely, more or less, what the people who created them set out to create. If we look only at the empirical correlation and set aside the basic reality that all of these things are man-made by deliberate will and decision, then we are on a very narrow and arid path."

The freedoms may well spread across national borders by diffusion or because of systems of interest or because of strong individual wills, but Stephen Post was convinced that democratic freedoms are fundamentally "related to the presuppositions of Judeo-Christianity. We may not be conscious of those presuppositions. They're like the air we breathe: we're not aware of the fact that we're breathing it—we just do. One goes back to the Pauline texts and their emphasis on freedom and equality. And if one looks at the very earliest church in its first several decades, and at aspects of Benedict's Rule, where there are strong democratic elements, and if one looks at Milton, who was inspired by the left wing of the Puritan Reformation, and if one looks at the American congregationalists, who insisted that anything and everything had to be done on the basis of election and election only, there seems to be an impulse in the tradition of Judeo-Christian ideas that leads toward democracy. This impulse is an explosive force that opens up society."

Peter Berger was skeptical. His skepticism was based, in part, on the counterexample of Japan, where democracy seems to be thriving in a non–Judeo-Christian society.

But Post countered the counterexample. "My father-in-law lives on a rice farm in Japan. He tells me that they have a very difficult time with democracy in Japan. Now there's a tremendous movement back in the direction of emperor worship. There's a very significant political movement to try to somehow return to the old, autocratic ways. So I'm not sure that Japan represents anything more than a momentary Westernization."

"I agree," said Gastil. "The democratic success in Japan is shallow. But that doesn't mean that Japan hasn't made some progress toward having a stable basis for democracy and can't achieve it in the future."

Rights, Related and Ranked

The conferees had been considering the extension of freedoms around the globe. Now James Nuechterlein wanted to consider the extension of freedoms in American society. "The American extension of the franchise—that is, the political freedom to vote—depended in part on a commitment to economic rights and freedoms. The extension of the democratic franchise was related to economic freedom because it was assumed, by society's elite, that the nation could afford democracy. Why? Because the franchise was not seen as an economic threat."

"Boy, were they wrong!" Berger joked, as several joined him in laughter.

Gastil picked up on Nuechterlein's point: "There's an imminent reason within democratic systems for the extension of the franchise. That is, there will always be a part of the political leadership in whose interest it will be to extend the franchise. And within the ideology of democracy, there is the idea of equality, which has in it the idea that everybody is equal and therefore should be enfranchised. The person who wants to extend the franchise always has a good argument on his side. The other side doesn't have a good argument, so even if its interests are going to be hurt, it finds it hard to resist the move to extend the franchise.

"Historically, then, the franchise was extended steadily in the United States, and then it was extended in every other democracy in the world, very often by directly copying what had happened in a neighboring state. That happened in countries all over Europe, many of which didn't identify with England."

The next speaker, Professor Martin Golding of the School of Law at Duke, began a different line of inquiry. "When I was a high-school student in the 1940s," he said, "I had a teacher who was a communist, although he said he wasn't a member of the Communist Party. He used to contrast the United States with the Soviet Union by saying that in this country we have political freedom but we don't have economic freedom, whereas the Soviet Union has no political freedom but has economic freedom. This made me very suspicious of the notion of economic freedom. In fact, I find that the term 'freedom' itself is problematic. I have less trouble with the term 'freedoms.'"

Furthermore, Golding asked, "why is the notion of political freedoms clearer, as Dr. Gastil suggested, than the notion of religious freedoms; and why is the notion of religious freedoms clearer than the notion of economic freedoms? What is the source?"

Neuhaus, briefly exchanging the moderator's mantle for

a participant's, responded to Golding. "That gets us into Isaiah Berlin's idea of positive and negative freedom. Also, as Kent Hill reminded us, the discourse in this room is not representative of the discourse about these questions in our society and our churches. There are many people, certainly in the SDS-style New Left, who would say that political freedom is by no means as clear as Gastil would say it is, and that real political freedom is something like full participation or participatory democracy. They would also say that what we have is not political freedom at all but simply a procedural sham whereby people are deceived into thinking that they're exercising power when they're not. So the descending order of clarity could be stood on its head."

Gastil begged to differ: "There have been surveys of political and civil rights in the world other than the survey done by Freedom House. What is notable about them, even when they're done by people far to the Left, is that they come up with almost the same kind of results. In other words, by and large, people across a very large spectrum don't disagree that much on political rights and religious liberties. But they do disagree on economic rights."

Speaking up for a certain understanding of economic rights, Joachim Maitre suggested a case study. "Let's look very briefly at Chile. This will show very clearly the extent to which our Western societies have become positively biased against economic rights, as compared with our very positive bias in favor of political rights. Right now Chile has—and this is the best-kept secret in the Western world—the only thriving economy in the hemisphere, far ahead of those of other countries." Maitre argued that Chile's economy is thriving because several key sectors of the economy—the national forests, agriculture, and mining—have been privatized. "Chile has a very successful economic model to offer. We ignore it at our own risk, and we are likely to ignore it because we're much more interested in liberalizing politics."

Neuhaus deduced and suggested that Maitre wanted to rank economic freedoms above political freedoms.

But how can economic freedoms be given priority, asked Gastil, when it's not clear what the economic freedoms are? "After all," he continued, "we don't have a meeting of the minds, even in this room, on the terms of economic freedom, as far as what should be allowed and what shouldn't be allowed. I suspect that around this table there would be a lot of disagreement even on the issue of the privatization of the forests. There just isn't that kind of disagreement in the arena of political freedoms or even in the arena of religious freedoms."

Then Berger responded to Maitre's remarks on Chile. "As far as the facts on Chile are concerned, Professor Maitre is correct. What's happening economically in Chile is incredible. Many people don't want it to be true because they don't like the regime. A parallel, by the way, is Taiwan. Taiwan, which is one of the most important cases of economic development in the post–World War II era, is invisible to many people basically because of ideological reasons.

"Professor Maitre is suggesting a thesis that was held in the 1950s by a good many development theorists in the United States who were not at all sympathetic to dictatorships. The thesis is that dictatorship can be a better guardian of successful economic development than democracy, because democracy introduces all sorts of social conflicts that a dictatorship can suppress. So if a dictatorship pursues economically rational policies, and that obviously is a big 'if,' then it is preferable to democracy at a certain stage of economic growth. Then, according to this thesis, it would be better to introduce capitalist development policies and implement democracy later, rather than the other way around."

Last of all, Berger editorialized, "I have no philosophical problem with accepting such a thesis. Again, it wouldn't trouble me if this were true. I'm not a religious believer in democracy. But I think the evidence is a little more complicated. I'm unconvinced by this thesis. Let me give you a few concrete cases where there has been very successful economic development under the auspices of democratic regimes—post–World War II Japan, Malaysia, Sri Lanka, and the Punjab in India. I'll stick with my strongly supportable thesis that you can't have democracy without a base of capitalist development, but I'm not sure that you can make the statement that in order to have democracy, you first have to have economic success."

Neuhaus then asked the group a very provocative question: "Is there any situation that one could imagine, in terms of a place in the world or in terms of a concept, where economic development or capitalism would work against political development or democracy?"

"In theory or in fact?" Gastil inquired.

"In theory *or* in fact," Neuhaus answered.

"In theory I can imagine anything," Berger postulated.

"Okay. Then only in fact," Neuhaus qualified.

"South Africa," replied Andrew Sullivan. "There capitalism entrenches the success of the political elite, and it gives them more economic and political power to use against reform."

Neuhaus disagreed: "In South Africa I think the economic factor is the strongest force for democratization. It's one thing the apartheid regime won't be able to resist."

Martin Golding then observed that "at some point in the discussion we switched from the term 'economic freedom' to the term 'economic development.' There may be a connection between the two, but they are distinguishable."

Sullivan wasn't deterred by Golding's distinction. Opposing Maitre's thesis, he said, "Here I speak as a non-American. It seems so obvious to this society and to this culture that economic freedom, political freedom, and religious freedom should be so intrinsically linked. But that really isn't the case for any other nation outside of the United States. Therefore, the argument that somehow a dictator will or can or should, because of economic success, liberalize politically is a very dangerous argument. I don't see the logic in that. For example, one thinks of Nazism as a classic case of a capitalist economic structure that progressively became aggressively antidemocratic." South Africa is a similar case, he argued.

"Only in America, says Sullivan, does this linkage among the freedoms exist," reiterated Neuhaus.

"That's correct," said Sullivan. "Not even in England."

Then both Neuhaus and Maitre reminded the conferees that Nazism in Germany was and is represented as national *socialism*, not as national *capitalism*.

In fact, Rabbi Novak asserted, "national socialism clearly saw Bolshevism as the problem that could destroy civilization and saw capitalism as impotent to do anything about it. National socialism, therefore, was clearly anti-capitalist in its rhetoric. Capitalism, according to national socialism, was the Weimar Republic. So Hitler seduced the capitalist class and then in the end did them in. Interestingly enough, the only almost-successful opposition to Hitler came very late in the war from precisely capitalist landowning classes that saw themselves as being totally destroyed by him."

Before the term "economic development" dropped out of the discussion, Berger wanted to make sure it was satisfactorily described. "Successful economic development has two features. The first is sustained economic growth. The second is distribution—that is, broad masses of people participate in the benefits of that economic growth. It isn't successful economic development if you have a very small elite gathering all of the benefits while most people continue to starve."

Beyond the Solitary Self

Detecting some unargued political-philosophical assumptions in the discussion, Francis Canavan intervened: "I wonder whether we can discuss rights simply in terms of rights and the balancing of rights. And should we take freedom simply as a good in itself and as an end in itself, without reference to something above both rights and freedom for the sake of which you want specific rights and whatever degree of freedom you're looking for? With regard to economic freedoms, I suppose you could defend them on utilitarian grounds. They seem to bring about greater economic growth and more production and perhaps better distribution. But this is something quite different from seeing them as rooted in the nature of the individual.

"Raymond Gastil speaks of society's identification of the individual as the ultimate human value. The word 'individual,' however, begs certain questions. One could use other terms. Individuality is a term of distinction and separation. It means, 'I am me and not you.' You could say 'human being' or 'the person' or 'the bearer of human nature,' all of which are terms that are common. If you use them, you're going to wind up with rather different conclusions about rights and freedoms. What I'm suggesting is that underlying this whole question of rights and freedoms is the question of human nature—what a human being is and what is good for him. Those are, of course, highly disputed questions. But I don't think we can achieve a solution to them by saying, 'Let's not answer them, let's be neutral.'

"Whatever individualism is, it's not a neutral term. It definitely reflects a position. It's right out of liberal political theory. There's no doubt about it. As Peter Berger said in one of his articles, 'Modern consciousness has perceived the solitary self as the bearer of human dignity,' and so indeed it has. But I think the situation we're running into today indicates we have to question that. We have to question whether we can take the human being as the solitary self and say that the good society is the one that frees the solitary self up to the point where it begins to get into its own way and operate against itself; after all, some solitary selves are going to get more than others."

"So, Dr. Gastil is a Millsian ideologue," Neuhaus kidded.

Gastil, always the good sport, claimed that he could use the term "individual" without pushing individualism. He continued, "One can build up a picture of the democratic community and democratic rights based on the idea of the ultimate indivisibility of individuals. That can mean that the community has certain rights vis-à-vis individuals. These rights present the possibility for democratic community to have many controls over other aspects of life, as a consequence of looking at the individual in that way. The way I'm using the term 'individual' here lays the basis for deciding against the idea of absolute individual rights."

At this point Neuhaus said to Gastil, "I'm troubled by your notion that individual rights and collective rights are pitted against each other and that there are trade-offs. I'm not sure that conceptually that's right."

Canavan reinforced and deepened Neuhaus's objection: "I don't think you get anywhere by talking about balancing the rights of the community with the rights of the minority or the individual unless there's some higher stand by which to decide what those rights are.

"As Berger reminded us, the terms 'liberal' and 'democracy' aren't synonymous. They may even be antithetical. A democracy, after all, can be highly communitarian, and liberalism is, of course, an individualistic doctrine. You can have a conception of community, such as Robert Nozick's, where the community is a collection of individuals and where there is no social entity of the common good for the sake of which you can ask any individual to make a sacrifice. All that can happen in that kind of community is that you can ask some individuals to sacrifice for other individuals. That's a purely liberal, individualistic conception of what a community is. Others would say that the community is something more than just the sum total of the individuals, that the good of the community is more than the sum total of individual goods, that there is such a thing as the common good. That's the kind of question you have to face before you can really talk consistently about rights."

"Yes, there is a common, community interest that exists separately from the interests of the individuals and from the interests of majorities," Gastil agreed. "But in a political system, what you come down to in the end is this: Who defines what that common interest is? On an individual-by-individual basis, the majority essentially defines what that is."

Jim Finn then joined the discussion: "In the example of the ten people living on the island, Dr. Gastil talks about the minority of four being oppressed. But if you have an idea of the common good—at least if it's shared by all ten people on the island—what they understand is that they're voting on something for the common good, even if they as individuals lose the vote, and what they're determining is how that common good will be arrived at. But they won't consequently feel oppressed even if they're in the minority. With this sense of the common good, democracy can't be reduced to a contest of individual against individual and majority against minority. In the island example there is a common good, which is the salvation of all of them—not the majority, not the minority, but all of them."

Neuhaus followed with this comment: "There isn't a trade-off in Raymond's ten-on-an-island example. The fact that the ten have agreed on how they're going to decide about the common good assumes something more than procedure has been decided on with regard to the relationship among them. How did they arrive at that agreement? They voted. That's a most unlikely way to make that decision. After all, couldn't the biggest bully among them just steal all the money and go out to buy an airplane, or whatever? But the ten decided that they were going to abide by an artificial thing called an election. This surely assumes that something more has gone on here.

"The important thing," Neuhaus concluded, "is that there's an agreement on the procedure for deciding. This means that nobody loses, even when the decision goes against one side."

Gastil's agreement was less than enthusiastic. "Some of us agree that there is a kind of innate justice in democratic arrangements based on the idea of one man, one vote. Many communities, given the opportunity, will make that choice, and they have historically."

Kenneth A. Myers, an author and editor, then asked the communitarian question, or questions. "As I was reading through these essays, I saw very little of the concept of duty, which does seem to be a correlative idea of the idea of rights and freedoms. When you talk about the common good, you have to ask, What is common? That is, how extensive is the community that you're defining? That relates to the question of duty because the idea of duty is defined by the community one belongs to. When you talk about the island people, I want to ask, Who are the ten people? How are they related? Why are they there? What is the nature of their community? I don't want to see them as just ten individuals."

Before and during the discussion of the common good, Frithjof Bergmann had noticed two competing ideas of freedom. He elaborated: "One is simply the idea that you are free when the government or the state is in no position or is in a limited position to interfere with you. The other is the idea that you are free to the extent to which there are no obstacles in your way and you can do what you want. From this point of view there isn't much difference between a police officer being able to say to you, 'You can't go into this movie theater,' and somebody else who isn't an agent of the state saying to you, 'We don't hire people who look like you, who talk like you, who smell like you.'

"In the political sphere we have defined freedom in terms of the non-interference of the state. Take the example of free speech. It makes sense to think of free speech as being able to say what you want in certain contexts without having to go to prison. But if you want to introduce the notion of being able to say anything you want without any interference, no matter how stupid your statement is, that notion would become absurd and empty. This shows that there is some real justification for linking freedom of speech to non-interference from the state.

"In the economic sphere, because of the trade-offs involved—plant closings, for example—one doesn't want to talk only about non-interference from the state. One wants to talk about the broader notion of freedom—that is, having no obstacles in one's way. Freedom here would mean the possibility of working if one wants to work, or the possibility of making a decent income if one works. These things don't lend themselves very well to the simple notion of the non-interference of the state.

"So, why is the notion of economic freedom so confusing and puzzling to us? Possibly because these two different notions of freedom conflict with each other. One group of people thinks of economic freedom in terms of non-interference from the state—that is, no taxation, no restrictions on property rights, no restrictions on possible commercial transactions. The other group tends to think of economic freedom in terms of the more encompassing notion of no obstacles. So the two different groups have two different conceptions of economic freedom, and thus they cannot communicate. Consequently, people become confused."

Bergmann, believing that identifying freedom with non-interference of the state is both dubious and narrow, concluded, "You can do one of two things to enable a person to overcome obstacles and thus make a person freer: either lower the obstacles or empower the person to jump higher or longer."

"I have no problem with the broad definition that you seem to endorse," Peter Berger responded. "But let's put it in inelegant language: All kinds of institutions can screw me— true, not only the state. However, if I then ask this question— Under modern conditions, which institution is most likely to screw me and screw me thoroughly with power at its disposal that no other institution has?—I get back to the state. The reason why one focuses on the state doesn't have to do with some definitional question; it simply has to do with the power of the state to create enormous obstacles."

Bergmann, ironically, played the part of the sociologist in response: "I guess that depends very much on your social background and what your position is and the way you make a living. In our lives the thing that screws us the most may be the state, although I'm not sure about that. I sometimes think that role is played by my colleagues more than the state. My point is that defining freedom only in terms of non-interference by the state is very much open to question."

Substantive Procedure and the Self

Once again, David Novak returned the group to Raymond Gastil's island-people example. "Irrespective of anybody's theory of rights, all such theories are based upon some notion of the good. Rights can always be shown to be a subset of the good. Even in classical contractual rights theory, where basically an individual contracts with society, the individual is seen to be or to possess good, and rights are a claim that he makes upon society in the interest of his individual good.

"This theory contrasts with a covenantal model of society, where the very participation in the commonality of society is itself a good. It isn't simply a claim that I make on other people. It's something I regard as good, something to be done. If that is our model of rights, if rights are basically freedoms for fulfilling personhood *in the context of commonality,* then the four people in Dr. Gastil's illustration who were outvoted on the boat-plane issue wouldn't regard themselves as being screwed by the majority. Why? Simply because the good of being a part of the commonality overrides their private versions of what is good. That, of course, would mean that the only type of society to which one could make that kind of commitment is one that is truly open to free discourse. If one begins with all goods being private and individual, then one is always going to regard the state or society as being nothing but a threat that has to be constantly overcome. In other words, society itself will have no positive value, and all will be diminished as a consequence."

Neuhaus then commented, "David, you're challenging

the usual distinction between the procedural and the substantive by saying that the procedural itself can, to the extent that it tends to preserve a community of a shared understanding of the good, be a substantive good."

"Precisely," Novak replied. "Procedure isn't just a means for bargaining for my own private good. I consider the good of being part of a community that accepts diversity of opinion and participation to be a good that I myself recognize as being greater than my own private opinion."

At this juncture Gastil responded to Novak: "You could have a much more generalized understanding of majoritarian rights. For example, everybody on that island might have gone there separately just the week before the vote, having no relationship to each other whatsoever. But if they were good Americans, they would, after having taken the vote, have accepted the idea that the majority had certain rights because they had accepted that procedural principle. In other words, you can accept this procedural approach at a much lower level of assumption about community than Dr. Novak seems to be making."

"But you're making what I consider to be the error of somebody like John Rawls," Novak continued. "Granted, there are societies where we just arrived yesterday or the day before. But for the most part, we're part of communities that have long, long histories; we're not simply recent arrivals on the island. Because of that, there are lots of aspects of commonality that have already been built up. I would regard your scenario of everybody having recently arrived on the island as a rather atypical example of society."

At this point Andrew Sullivan jumped to the defense of Rawls. "John Rawls asserts that he isn't making any great metaphysical claims about the person. He's simply saying that we can sit down, even with great histories and communities, and agree to play a game that seems compatible with certain innate and intuitive senses about justice."

Unconvinced, Ken Myers asked, "Are there some communities in which that kind of game would be considered blasphemous or irreverent? For example, even to suggest that I ignore, say, the fact that my father is my father would be very offensive to many communities."

Sullivan responded, "Rawls would say, 'Yes, that's true. However, I'm only addressing the modern, American, liberal-political tradition.' So, there have to be *Americans* on the island." Some laughter followed.

Next Stephen Post made it clear that he isn't a devotee of Rawlsian individualism: "Rawls makes an enormous mistake in discussing justice by utterly ignoring the family. All Enlightenment and post-Enlightenment moral philosophy, whether we're talking about the Kantian or the utilitarian strains, has a philosophy of the self that strips it of all essential social and biological embodiments. In such philosophies family doesn't count. Special relationships, such as friendship, don't count. Veils of ignorance and island scenarios mistakenly create what Alasdair MacIntyre correctly calls a very ghostly and abstract view of the self. That is a tremendous problem. We have no theory of justice or moral philosophy that takes up filial morality—what parents owe children, what wife owes husband and vice versa, and so on."

"But what about the claim that such veils and scenarios are nevertheless useful thought exercises?" Neuhaus asked Post.

Post was ready: "They are, but they still give you an unduly Enlightenment-oriented, fairly ethereal view of the self that's probably more appropriate for Kant's notion of a numinous being and an angel than for somebody who's actually alive and in this world. So we don't have a framework in which to think about what we owe each other. We think about justice almost like a gravitational field where there is no gravity, so every planet pulls equally on every other planet no matter how remote and distant it might be. This is a terrible mistake in Enlightenment thought."

"So, not only are such scenarios not especially useful, but they can be downright harmful?" Neuhaus quizzed.

"Yes, they can be downright harmful," Post agreed.

Too Much Democracy?

When the conferees returned to the issue of majoritarian rights, Mary Ann Glendon of Harvard Law School observed that "a lot depends on the issues that come up for majority vote.

For example, should matters of religious conscience come up for majority vote? In this country there is a strong notion that religious matters and certain other things cannot come up for a vote. Specified individual rights are not subject to being bargained away—although it is true in some sense, as Hobbes says, that every man has his price and will bargain away anything, even his religious conscience, for certain other goods. So, whether or not people feel oppressed by a vote depends in large part on what it is that's up for a vote."

Neuhaus then related Glendon's comment to the island scenario. "In the island scenario, we're concerned with what is being decided. Yes, the subject matter of the decision is critically important. In the illustration it's a purely instrumental decision because the agreement is that everybody wants to get off the island and at issue is the best technique for doing that. The real crunch comes when you start making decisions in which people feel impinged upon or, as some say, oppressed."

Francis Canavan got at the same issues by using a different approach—American jurisprudence. "There's a phrase that the U.S. Supreme Court has become fond of—'ordered liberty.' I don't like what the Court is getting out of it, but I think that the phrase in itself is a good one. There really is no such thing as liberty. Any liberty has to fit into some larger order of things. Liberty, then, depends upon an order and is intelligible only as part of an order. In discussing questions of liberty, we're making sense only if we're asking about order and the ordering principle of which we want our liberties to be a part.

"Now one can conceptualize an order, as Kant did, which consists of nothing but a framework in which everybody has an equal box in which he can do whatever he wants. The only limit is that nobody can go over to somebody else's box and interfere with his liberty. So the order is one that simply guarantees equal liberty to all, and the only function of the state is to maintain the lines between the boxes.

"That would be an order of a sort. But I don't think it has much relevance to anything in the world. The only people who would want that, I suspect, are intellectuals. In the real world people are always thinking about other social goods and what they want to obtain. I don't mean to say that they are therefore voting for totalitarianism. It's a peculiar myth which says that you have to choose either a radical individualism or totalitarianism. In the real world the spectrum of choice is infinitely wider than that.

"So when you talk about liberty, you have to talk about the order of human social goods in which you're going to fit liberty. You have to ask, How will the goods impinge upon liberty, and what effect will the exercise of liberty have upon these goods? Those are the terms with which people are inclined to think. When they vote in an election, they may be voting with their wallets in mind much more than with their conceptions of the Bill of Rights, and who's to say they're necessarily wrong?"

"That's a rather chic statement," charged Joachim Maitre.

"Well, take your own position, the Austrian school of economics," Canavan replied to Maitre. "Hayek says that economic liberty produces spontaneous order. To that I would say, Great!—if indeed it does. And it darned well better if you want people to consent to it. There has to be an order, and a livable order, that grows out of the exercise of economic liberty. Society will start to limit economic liberty when it sees that liberty beginning to frustrate greater goods."

Michael Warder of The Rockford Institute cast Glendon's concern about raw majoritarianism in terms of "the overabundance of democracy." It's possible, he said, "that you can have too much democracy, if it begins to impinge upon freedom. Suppose, for example, that the ten people on the island had to vote on what kind of hammers to use. In other words, the process starts to get mucked up if so much has to be put to a vote all the time that some people decide not to vote because they get tired of it and they figure that voting is useless anyway. I raise this point because there's a question about how democracy supports freedom. Democracy can grind down freedom. One of the problems in the United States now is that when there are elections, very few people vote, and yet decisions are made that affect the whole society. So maybe democracy can— if it's bad democracy—diminish freedom."

That comment took Neuhaus back to the notion of participatory democracy. "Some would say that style of democracy is too much democracy," he said. "Others would say that it's undemocratic, because it doesn't respect those things that aren't up for majority vote. Democratic totalitarianism is certainly undemocratic."

Raymond Gastil tied the subject under discussion to American democracy: "There has been a general disillusionment with democracy in the United States. What I've been most struck by is that the New England town meeting, which in fact decides the issues for the towns in many rural areas of New England, is getting only about 8 to 10 percent attendance at best, even on budgetary issues. The reason given by the people who stay away is that their attendance doesn't make any difference. But in fact it does make a difference; they could turn around any one of those meetings if they attended. But for some reason they're turned off by the process."

"Then again," hypothesized Neuhaus, "a lot of them might be quite satisfied with the decisions being made."

"Not to hear them talk. Apparently they're not satisfied. They think somebody else is running the town," Gastil retorted.

Glendon then passed along an observation gained from experience: "As an attender of New England town meetings for many, many years and as the daughter of a selectman, I can see that one of the reasons people today feel it doesn't matter anymore is that there are fewer issues decided at the local level. Today so much is subject to federal and state regulation. There is a great loss of control."

With that observation the first day of the conference drew to a close. Although all of the questions raised by the idea of the good hadn't been answered, many had been energetically engaged during this session.

THE PRIORITY OF RELIGIOUS FREEDOM

On the morning of the second day of the conference, moderator Neuhaus introduced the third presenter tongue-in-cheek: "I give you George the Weigel."

Weigel, formerly of the James Madison Foundation and now of the Ethics and Public Policy Center, began, "I'm going to fly very quickly through the argument of my essay to refresh your memories and, most importantly, my own. Then I'll be eager for the conversation that follows."

Weigel proceeded to make good on his promise. He concluded his summary with this comment: "John Paul II's argument for the priority of religious freedom in the scheme of human rights and his connection of religious freedom to the democratic project is cast in personalist, natural-law terms that make the claims accessible beyond the boundaries of the Roman Catholic Church. His argument isn't cast in particularist, Catholic language and concepts. That's a deliberate and well-made choice."

Freedom of Conscience, Freedom of Religion

Neuhaus was the first to note that Weigel assumes that freedom of conscience is equivalent to freedom of religion and that that assumption is not necessarily an acceptable one.

Gastil agreed with Neuhaus and then added a footnote: "Historically, the appearance of the other freedoms we talked about preceded the appearance of the freedom of conscience. If you go through history, at the beginning you find a religion-state combination—for example, in ancient Greece and in Socrates—such that it was treasonous to be against state religion. Then you find the development of certain secular ideas about political and civil freedoms which gradually included religious freedom. In the United States, for example, at the time of the Revolutionary War, there still were considerable controls of a religious nature, even in New England. Those controls—in Massachusetts, for example—weren't lifted until the 1830s, long after all of the other controls on civil liberties had been lifted.

"Therefore, it seems that the modern interpretations of religious liberty are, in some sense, by-products of something else that was happening in the secular world. The secular world was liberalizing, and this was accepted as the basis of religious life. This included the freedom of the individual conscience and the freedom of the minority in the community to believe what it wanted."

"Exactly what would the term 'secular world' mean in the sixteenth century?" Neuhaus wondered.

"Well, many of the thinkers of that time weren't primarily

occupied with religious questions," Gastil answered. "Francis Bacon, for example. And Thomas Jefferson." Neuhaus had further questions about the alleged secularity of the sixteenth century, but in the interest of time he didn't press them.

Francis Canavan also saw a difference between the freedom of conscience and the freedom of religion. "If you look at the definition of religious freedom in the Vatican II declaration," he said, "you'll notice that it doesn't use the phrase 'freedom of conscience.' The human *person* has a right to religious freedom—the *person* rather than the *conscience*.

"In the aftermath of the French Revolution, the Roman Catholic Church was at war with the liberal-secular state and the state's doctrine of the supremacy of the individual conscience, which is based on individualism. The church hadn't then accepted this individualism, and it hasn't to this day. In the twentieth century, faced with the rise of the totalitarian state and its contempt for religious man, the church simply turned around—it didn't change its ground—and faced another direction and began to insist upon a doctrine of human rights. But I don't think it's correct to say that the church therefore accepted the conception of the liberal-individualist state and its freedom of conscience."

To this Weigel responded, "The declaration doesn't use the term 'freedom of conscience' for all the reasons you suggest. But John Paul II does, even in *Redemptor Hominis,* which can be taken as program notes for his ministry. Now, if there's anything we can say with certainty about John Paul II, it is that he isn't a French liberal of the eighteenth-century individualist stripe. So I'm interested in why that term is now in play at that level. I suspect that 'freedom of conscience' is such a loose term that a lot of stuff can be poured into it. But in a limited sense it surely means that one shouldn't be coerced about matters of ultimate concern. That, in secular language, describes what we're talking about here."

At this point Peter Berger offered a different slant on the freedom-of-conscience/freedom-of-religion question: "It occurs to me that freedom of conscience and freedom of religion could be antagonistic to each other. This goes back to Phyllis Zagano's idea that religion could actually be corroded because of democracy, because of democratic liberties. First I think one should differentiate between the way in which democratic liberties affect particular religious traditions and the way in which they affect what for the moment I will hesitantly call 'the religious attitude.'

"Specific religious traditions, I'm sure, are challenged by the pluralistic situation that a democratic regime doesn't produce but certainly institutionalizes and legitimates. Whereas through most of human history most people lived in communities with one organized religious worldview, we now live in a situation where different religious worldviews and nonreligious worldviews constantly rub shoulders. This situation undermines religious certainties. So, from the point of view of specific religious traditions—for example, if I'm a Roman Catholic or a Jew or a Muslim or whatever—the democratic situation doesn't cause problems, but it institutionalizes problems that modernization brings about anyway.

"But if one talks about the religious attitude—and I'm not sure that that's the right phrase to use—I think we're dealing with a different situation. We're dealing with what a philosopher friend of mine calls 'metaphysical space'— space left in social life for experiences of awe and wonder, which may or may not have a transcendent dimension in the religious sense, but which Sidney Hook or Albert Camus are capable of. This came out dramatically in debate on the issue of whether a few moments of observed silence in a public-school classroom does or does not violate the First Amendment. It struck me as a kind of madness that anyone should think that a few moments of silence violate the disestablishment clause of the U.S. Constitution. What is silence? It is the opposite of noise. To suggest that, in the noise of social life, we should for a moment stop and be quiet is not to promote a particular religion. It is to promote a fundamental, human attitude that opens up the possibility for the expression of the metaphysical dimensions of the human condition. That is not corroded or attacked by the pluralistic situation.

"The challenge to religious traditions that comes from modern pluralism is a very healthy challenge. As far as Christianity is concerned, it takes us right back to the beginning, where Christianity was one sect among many. This makes us relatively free of the Constantinian event in Christian history. And I certainly think that from the particularistic point of view one should welcome the silence which recalls the metaphysical dimension of human existence. So, freedom of religion and freedom of conscience are different and in a sense antagonistic, but in the end, from any particularistic point of view, they are affirmed together."

Later in the discussion, hypothetically playing the part of a Buddhist monk, Berger illlustrated his point. "Why do I say that American democracy is such a very positive event for religion? Because, unlike other political structures of the modern world—of which the totalitarian state is the worst—the democratic state leaves open the possibility of religious enlightenment. It doesn't cause it—it isn't qualified to cause it. But it leaves open that possibility. For me, freedom of conscience has a very broad foundation that isn't in fundamental tension with my particular tradition. Ultimately freedom of conscience can affirm my faith."

Christian Totalitarianism

Next Berger sketched a scenario that set off a long and thoughtful exchange. His story went like this: "Suppose that Mikhail Gorbachev became converted by Aleksandr Solzhenitsyn. Gorbachev decided not only that the totalitarian state could survive while allowing people to do their own religious thing but also that the totalitarian process would be completed by having one religious foundation, which might well be Russian Orthodoxy. That's a frightening thought."

"People who know the Soviet Union very well," replied George Weigel, "tell me that there have been secret baptisms up to and including the Central Committee. There's something resembling a religious renaissance gurgling beneath the crust of Soviet life."

Liah Greenfeld agreed. "There is indeed a religious revival reported by the Communist Party, or by the followers of the Party, in the Soviet Union. It is a revival, especially of the Russian Orthodox Church, that now performs the function of the new assertion of Russian nationalism. But this doesn't change anything!"

"But my question is, Would the Soviet Union become less totalitarian or more totalitarian when all its citizens became baptized?" Berger reiterated.

Or, as Neuhaus put it, "Are Christian totalitarians more to be feared than atheistic totalitarians?"

"The Soviet Union has allowed genuine religious freedom," said Kent Hill. "It did in the 1920s. Then it gave relative freedom to the evangelicals, hoping that that would split or hurt the Orthodox Church. The growth was so astounding that it finally had to treat the Orthodox and the Protestants alike. Why? Because in the Soviet Union there is an incredible sense of boredom. Marxism is unable to meet people's basic needs, and this makes the people very curious about religion, even if they're ill-informed about it."

Hill went on, defining some of the terms of the discussion. "Also, we need to remember that if a totalitarian state were to allow religious freedom, it would no longer really be a totalitarian state. Totalitarianism means precisely the attempt to control every aspect of life. If you take religion out of that formula, then you move back to an authoritarian state of one sort or another. Thus you cannot have a totalitarian state with religious freedom.

"Well, is there a danger of Christian totalitarianism? Again, I'm concerned about our use of terms. One could make a very strong case that 'Christian totalitarianism' is an oxymoron, that it is intellectually impossible. To the extent that something emerged which called itself Christian and totalitarian, to that extent the term 'Christian' would be heretically used. Since Christianity has made much of human dignity, and since human dignity is irreconcilable with the totalitarian state, you can't put Christianity and totalitarianism together. Also, there's something about the paradox of the created order that requires freedom which allows for the possibility of people making the wrong choices. That's precisely what totalitarianism won't tolerate. In *The Brothers Karamazov* the Grand Inquisitor challenges Christ on this very point. He says, 'You did not love human beings sufficiently; you gave them too much freedom; we need to deprive them of their freedom in order to feed and house them properly.' In other words, there is a fundamental conflict between the Christian agenda and the totalitarian temptation."

"You're saying that Christian totalitarianism is heretical Christianity, but that Christians could do it," Neuhaus summarized.

"Sure," Hill said. "There are many similar cases in Christian history. Look at the theocracies of days gone by, which today tempt the Protestant 'theonomists.' But historically these people and groups were known as heretics."

Here Liah Greenfeld reminded the group of an oft-made claim: "Institutionally, it was the church, not the state, that was the main oppressor of the freedom of conscience. In the Middle Ages, if I recall correctly, only the church had the right to persecute for heresy. The state didn't have this right. We have to remember that the very important breakthrough toward liberal democracy started with the state. Henry VIII made the first successful state challenge of the control of the church."

Hill disagreed: "Others have said, as Professor Greenfeld has, that the church has been the source of intolerance and constraints on freedom of conscience. But I think that whatever progress we've seen in the area of freedom of conscience we can lay at the feet of the church. Whether you go back to A.D. 395, when Bishop Ambrose critiqued Emperor Theodosius for compelling religious belief, or to the worst cases in Christian history—the Inquisition, Geneva, or whatever—the remarkable thing is that the church has somehow limited its abuses. That's significant when you contrast it with the inability of secular ideologies to limit their abuses. There seems to be something inherent in Christianity that allows it to correct itself, even at its worst moments."

"John Bennett makes the point that the reason for that is the Christian doctrine of love," added Stephen Post.

Greenfeld had another explanation: "We can't forget the extraordinary strength of the modern state. The church never had at its disposal the power that any modern state has."

"The church could have done a lot more damage during the Inquisition than it did," countered Hill. "It had the power to kill a lot more people than it did."

Neuhaus then juxtaposed this historical horror with

others. "The Inquisition, in its three centuries of real operation, killed about as many people as were killed in a couple of hours on a busy afternoon either in the Third Reich or under Joseph Stalin. This is not to say that each death isn't an infinite outrage against human dignity, but it does help one to see things in perspective."

Instead of being worried about religious forms of totalitarianism and their sins, Dean Curry of Messiah College was concerned about religion becoming anemic and losing its ability to check an ever-expanding state. Curry explained: "In what practical, real sense can we say that notions of transcendence in fact place effective limits on state power today and thus constitute a source of democracy? I'm attracted to this idea, and if we look at the framers of the Constitution and at Tocqueville and at the early years of the American republic, we'll see that there was a sense of transcendence which manifested itself in a number of ways. But I'm not sure that it exists in a real way anymore in the current American context. Today the task of limiting state power is accomplished by a secularized political culture with little reference to religion. These secular limits are visceral, though Richard Neuhaus has suggested that they're genetic. The American people are committed to democracy, and their commitment is deep, thoroughgoing, and pervasive, but it isn't based on any explicit reference to transcendence."

Faith and/or Freedom

Rabbi David Novak wanted to make sure that religious freedom is unequivocally based on religion. Novak said to George Weigel, "I have a problem with what you do with Sidney Hook, because I don't see anything in Hook or those like him that affirms transcendent warrants for freedom. Basically, Hook— from what I've read of him—affirms that the human person transcends total state control. But he doesn't base that on a transcendent source. On the contrary, he would deny the transcendent source. Hook's or any individualist's notion of freedom forces my religious convictions to be individualistic, and that belies my whole notion of society, because Judaism isn't individualistic.

"That's why I think your neoconservativism has interfered a little bit with your political theology, George. Granted, most of us here are conservatives, and I can see why you like Sidney Hook. But I think you've overargued his legitimacy.

"Because of where Hook and others are coming from, they're not going to be able to constitute freedom with transcendent warrants. That, I suspect, is a project of all of us—that is, to give a more adequate constitution of democracy and freedom than the ones given by the secularists of this world."

Before Weigel had a chance to answer Novak, Andrew Sullivan posed another question. "George, are you first a religious person or a liberal? Is the truth of religion more important to you than the truth of freedom? Vatican II hasn't answered that question, and I think in some ways the Vatican II documents are problematic in their implications for the relation of religion and politics, and the priority of one over the other."

Neuhaus then called for clarification: "Andrew, are you questioning whether Vatican II does or does not say that one is committed to religious freedom because one is a serious Christian? It seems to me that that is the argument, that religious freedom follows from Christian conviction."

"That is the argument in Vatican II," Sullivan agreed. Then he went on: "Professor Berger welcomes pluralism as an opportunity for religion to develop. But the religion that engages pluralism will become a different kind of religion. I don't think that there's nothing at stake. Presumably the fact that the modern Roman Catholic Church is going back to early Christian influences in its liturgy and in its lay practices is a result of the church's grappling with pluralism.

"Allow me one more attempt at explaining this. Is 'the dignity of the human person'—and I'd like to know exactly where that phrase comes from and exactly what it means—just a code for the defense of liberalism in the twentieth century as the least evil? That may be a very important defense. On the other hand, it's not the same as the defense of the truth. If we confuse the defense of the truth with the defense of liberalism as the lesser of two critical evils, we may be involved in a very dangerous error."

"Some would say that it is precisely for the sake of the

truth that there has been a convergence which requires an affirmation of liberalism," contended Neuhaus.

"Yes," replied Sullivan, "but that statement depends not on Christianity but on a Millsian form of liberalism. That understanding isn't a Christian understanding. It's a liberal understanding."

"But Christianity is becoming," answered Neuhaus. "It's still in process. Still, this is an excellent set of questions."

Now it was Weigel's turn. "It's great fun being accused first of being a neoconservative and then of being a liberal." In response to Sullivan, Weigel continued, "I'm quite clear, in my own mind, about my deepest commitments. They're ecclesial, not political. In the contemporary Catholic elite world I think the danger is not that the phrase 'the dignity of the human person' becomes a code for the defense of liberalism but that it becomes a code for the defense of Marxism. But the problem remains the same."

Jim Finn put a different spin, as they say, on the faith-and-freedom issue. "When it was being debated whether Catholicism was compatible with democracy, John Courtney Murray said that that way of putting the question was wrong. He said that, for a Catholic, the question is, 'Is democracy compatible with Catholicism?' which assumes, of course, that Catholicism has truth claims prior to any democratic institutions. Part of Jacques Maritain's intellectual enterprise was also to try to relate religion to democracy. At times he made rather strained arguments in his attempts to support the assertion that democracy is in fact grounded in the gospel. According to Maritain, the Christian understanding for the basis of freedom is that you know certain things to be true. And one of the things you know to be true is that the other person has a right to his conscience and to the expression of his conscience in the civil order."

"Thus tolerance emerges precisely from a truth claim," Neuhaus postulated.

"Yes," replied Finn. "That is Maritain's argument, and I think it's a forceful argument."

"And it was John Locke's argument too," added Sullivan.

Then Weigel added, "The notion that the intellectual history which leads to present modern democratic arrangements begins only with Locke is simply wrong—it's historically wrong. There are long lines that go back considerably further and that even have to do with medieval life."

Taking a cue from Peter Berger's earlier emphasis, Richard Hutcheson began talking about institutions: "George Weigel is suggesting a separation of church and state by degree. He suggests that a moderate kind of separation would solve the church-state problem. We must remember that separation of church and state is an institutional concept in American history. It has to do with the separation of the institutional church and the institutional state, but not with the separation of religion and society. Therefore, the case of public funds for social goals channeled through religious institutions and the case of public funds to advance religious institutions are of different orders. The second is not valid under separation of church and state. The first has to do with the relationship of religion and society, and that is valid."

"They're different," Weigel agreed. "You're right. I think the priority should rest on the religion-and-society side. But one doesn't solve much of anything by saying that the First Amendment has to do only with institutional separation, because in our society we have many inextricable points of contact. And how do we sort them out, constitutionally and legally, whether in the areas of education or charitable organizations or whatever? For example, what do we do about vouchers, tax credits, government money running orphan homes of the Archdiocese of New York, and so on? That isn't settled simply by saying, 'Yes, there is institutional separation.'"

If Hutcheson was interested in institutions, then Stephen Post was interested in movements. Said Post, "I'm not certain that pluralism is taken as seriously as it should be in our democracy, and I'm not sure that the Catholic declarations on religious liberty go as far as they should. I say that for a couple of reasons. In American society there have emerged new religious movements. For example, traditional forms of Hinduism have sprung up on Eighth Avenue here in New York. These kinds of movements are dubbed 'cults,' and, as it has been argued, 'cult' is a word we use to define any religious or political movement that we don't like. That's fair enough. If you look at some of the history of American life over the last fifteen or twenty years, you'll find that it's highly ambiguous on the issue of pluralism. It seems to me that we're no better right now than we were with the Mormons in the 1800s. We haven't really stepped up a notch. The new pluralism is a threat to many. American society is not taking religious liberty as seriously as it should."

In his musings on faith, freedom, and the person, Weigel had made much of man's "quest for meaning and value." On this score Frithjof Bergmann had quite a bit to say. "The phrase 'quest for meaning and value' from Weigel's paper has an enormous sweep. It's a bit worn from overuse, but it still has great poetic power. To make that concrete, one might say that any number of writers would think of what they're writing in their novels or poetry or histories as a pursuit of meaning and value. One can even broaden the scope of the phrase. The purpose of all art, it can be said, is to somehow give meaning and value to life. And for many people who take their work seriously, whatever their work is, it represents a quest for meaning and value.

"Although I don't want to sound at all aristocratic or snobbish, I want to report that, in teaching, most professors know that the intensity of this quest is quite low among students. A lot of students don't have much of a sense of the quest for meaning and value. I'm reminded of Thoreau's phrase about the mass of men leading lives of quiet desperation. I think that many students, among others, do live lives of quiet desperation, primarily because they don't have much left of a quest for meaning and value.

"What are the factors or the obstacles that discourage people in their search for meaning and value? Well, there are many—from bad schools, to bad television, to the pressure to earn a living in a lousy job. So then one could say that there are some obstacles that the state puts in the way of people's quests for meaning and value. Totalitarianism is one danger-ous obstacle. Since I've lived under it, my credentials on that score are good. But there are other dangerous obstacles that discourage and dehumanize people. Contemporary conser-

vatism is in part definable by its preoccupation with the limitation of state obstacles. One of the differences between us is
that I think there's more to giving people freedom than just
limiting the state. In other words, after the state has been
limited, there's still much to be done in the quest for meaning
and value."

"Do we really 'give people freedom,' as you said?" Weigel
asked Bergmann.

"That was a slip," confessed Bergmann. "What I'm thinking is that we should envision and work toward the creation of
a society in which more freedom would become possible for
everyone."

Religious Liberty—How Large an Umbrella?

Martin Golding, the Duke professor of law and philosophy,
reminded the conferees of the unclear nature of religious liberty.
"People claim all sorts of things as religious matters, and people
in the public debate disagree over the scope of religious freedom. So it becomes important to determine the exact scope of
religious freedom. For example, some people in North Carolina
seem to think that basketball is a religion."

"But you're not coerced into being a Duke fan," Weigel
joked.

"Take a more serious example," urged Golding. "Take the
cases in the 1890s involving Mormons and polygamy. The language the courts used then stuns us today—'anti-Christian,'
'anti-religious,' 'demonic,' and so on. The claim that polygamy
is required by Mormonism was simply dismissed by the courts
as a virtually inconceivable notion."

"And laying mines in the Persian Gulf may be a religious
duty to some people," noted Ken Myers.

Neuhaus followed with a comment: "Religion, at least in
its Jewish and Christian versions, is totalistic in its claim to
bring the whole of life under obedience to God and his will.
Legally, in terms of First Amendment issues, the question then
becomes, What are the limits of free exercise? The answer is one
of continuing debate in a democratic society. But my own answer would involve an extremely broad space."

Nina Shea proceeded to highlight several violent examples of places where religious liberty does not exist. "In Chile there is freedom of worship, yet personnel in the archdiocese's office of social welfare in Santiago have been kidnapped, have disappeared, and have recently been brutalized by having crosses carved into their faces. Everybody believes these things were done by plainclothesmen related to the military. In South Africa, Catholic priests who preached and protested against apartheid were imprisoned and tortured for getting involved in that issue. In Guatemala, a Catholic priest was threatened with death, and both a religious school and a seminary that he founded were burned to the ground. Why? Because he was representing the Indian community and he was leading a movement for land reform.

"Also, in the Sandinista government in Nicaragua there were priests who were advancing liberation theology. Their theology embraced Marxist notions of class struggle rather than Christian love. There the state was at least designating and at most fostering church leaders, and at the same time delegitimating and expelling those priests who were not pro-Sandinista. In addition, there is the convergence of religious symbols with political ones—even to Che Guevara's being crucified on the cross. This is Peter Berger's nightmare—where religion will be used not just to advance nationalism, as in the Russian case, but to inculcate a totalitarian theory."

"Are you saying that even though freedom of religion, in the formal sense, may exist in Chile, South Africa, and Guatemala, it doesn't seem to have greatly enhanced democracy?" Berger asked Shea.

"No," Neuhaus answered, "I understand her to be saying that religious freedom doesn't exist, in the fullest definition of the Vatican Council, in those places. Yet people can worship there."

Then Shea spoke for herself. "But what if you believe that religion doesn't end with going to church on Sunday and that you should live out your religion? If apartheid violates your conscience, shouldn't you act on that?"

Berger then explained the reason behind his line of inquiry. "What George Weigel and I are maintaining is this: The opening to transcendence, which is certainly there if people are allowed to worship, is in some way conducive to democracy and to the limitation of the state. Your examples seem to say that it isn't."

"No, not at all, Peter," Neuhaus objected. "Because what you have in these examples are instances in which precisely the transcendent judgment which stands over against the state is motivating people to act in ways that bring them into conflict with the state. All of these examples demonstrate that transcendent religion isn't enough in the face of a powerful state that's prepared to resist and to do brutal things to people who are motivated by transcendent belief to establish democracy."

"In fact," argued Dean Curry, "in the case of South Africa, transcendence was used to squelch democracy."

"The state must see itself checked in some way by evidence of the transcendent," said Neuhaus. "But the state's simply being checked or restricted or restrained doesn't mean that it's going to move in a democratic direction."

Neuhaus went on to elaborate his point: "If the state permits a group of people to gather together and to say, 'Jesus Christ is Lord' or 'Sh'ma Israel,' that public event, which is tolerated by the state, relativizes the state. If Christ is Lord, Caesar is not. If there is one God, the state is not God. That has a relativizing effect, but it doesn't mean that the state is going to permit the communities of faith to act on the implications of their declarations of sovereignty. The state may say, 'You can say these things, but don't do anything about them that would threaten the government.' Indeed, most authoritarian states do exactly that. Totalitarian states, if they are successful, don't even permit the confession."

David Novak then focused attention on the authoritarian situation. "Because authoritarian states allow religious statements to be made in public, they will ultimately have to explain why and will have to move in one direction or the other. They can stop allowing those statements, or they can move toward religious freedom. As for the Jews in the Soviet Union, they did better under the authoritarian, czarist regime than under the consistently repressive Leninist regime."

Novak continued. "Dealing with a Christianized Marxism would provide more of an opening than dealing with a non-

Christianized Marxism, because Christianity would bring paradoxes that otherwise would not exist. Christianized Marxism would bring the possibility for change in the direction of freedom and democracy."

After Ken Myers noted that in this discussion the existence and activity of the Holy Spirit should be assumed, Neuhaus continued his exchange with Novak. "Liberation theology is powerfully insidious because of the way in which it empties theology of religious content and replaces it with political content, all the while maintaining a religious veneer. This is fundamentally a debasement of theology that eliminates all connection to authentic transcendence. That is the threat and the danger of liberation theology."

Curry agreed with Neuhaus: "Those doing the co-opting might seek to completely transform the message of God's transcendent truth into something purely secular, maintaining the outer shell of traditional religion—its language and themes—but destroying its transcendent essence. I believe this kind of transmutation has already begun to take place in Nicaragua, where the Sandinistas have encouraged the priests of the People's Church to use the language, stories, and themes of traditional Christianity while imbuing them with sectarian, secular meaning. For example, Nicaragua's liberation theologians preach a secular salvation—not an otherworldly spiritual salvation rooted in a transcendent reality but a political salvation gained through the Marxist revolution. Similarly, these theologians speak of humankind's need for a redeemer and savior and then identify him as a Marxist revolutionary.

"I affirm the importance of religion as a rampart against totalitarianism, and I agree that wherever and whenever God's word is spoken, it serves as a witness to transcendent truth. My concern is with ideological movements—such as some forms of liberation theology—that really have no interest in mixing Marxism with Christianity but simply wish to co-opt Christianity by utterly transforming its essentially transcendent message to serve their secular, totalitarian agendas. I fear that once this happens, there is little left to restrain the triumph of tyranny."

Novak refused to yield: "Still, even the People's Church

in Nicaragua, the church of liberation theology, holds out some hope for paradox. This hope, small though it might be, comes from the fact that the People's Church is part of the worldwide church. That connection with the worldwide church creates, or can create, an opening. So ecumenism keeps alive the possibility for paradox."

"Perhaps," said Neuhaus. "But we also have to remember that the Nicaraguan People's Church is a partisan church. It isn't interested in the worldwide church; it isn't interested in ecumenism. It is interested only in taking its place among the vanguard of history and fighting it out there until it is vindicated by the victory that it envisions."

The Church and the Nazis

Peter Berger then shifted the discussion to the case of the church in Nazi Germany. "With regard to the example of the German Christians, we should remember that Nazism in Germany didn't turn totalitarian until World War II. Up until then the Nazis weren't interested in taking over the church—for purely utilitarian reasons: they didn't think that taking over the church would do national socialism much good."

Rabbi Novak added to Berger's comment. "There are only two reasons for totalitarianism to attempt to use religion for its own purposes. First, totalitarianism can plunder cultural symbols from the religious groups of its society. The totalitarians' goal is to manipulate the meaning and message of these cultural symbols in order to increase their control of their society. The second totalitarian use of religion has to do with eschatological fervor. Since totalitarianism tends to lose its own eschatological enthusiasm, and since that enthusiasm is essential to the totalitarian project, it looks around for a supportive or a substitute eschatology. Often this can be found in religion. So, instead of squelching religion, totalitarianism sometimes tries to use religion for its own purposes in these two ways."

"Wait a minute," Berger urged. "We don't always need to see Machiavellian tendencies in the hearts and minds of totalitarians when we observe the ways they handle religion. Let's give them credit, sometimes. After all, I think some of them actually believe—actually believe!—their concoctions of religion and politics. Take, for example, Miguel d'Escoto, the priest and government official in Nicaragua. I think he actually believes what he says about liberation theology and the revolution."

At this juncture Andrew Sullivan reiterated the point Ken Myers had made earlier. "Christians and the mere existence of the church present to their societies the possibility of grace. And the possibility of grace always points to the possibility of change—even in societies, even in governments."

"That's certainly a strong faith claim," Neuhaus observed.

After this long discussion, in which the umbrella of religious liberty was assumed to be quite large, Raymond Gastil spoke up for a miniature version of the same umbrella. "Freedom of religion or freedom of conscience is best understood in a very narrow framework. Let's say we're talking about Poland and the efforts of the communist government there in relation to the church. The government's attempts to control the church with regard to matters of conscience were one thing; the government's attempts to control the church when the church sets itself up as a supporter of a particular political movement or as the defender of a trade union should be considered quite another. True, we can say that the conscience of the Polish Catholic demands that he go into these other areas, but that assertion starts to stretch the concepts. If we broaden freedom of religion and conscience to cover other areas, then we're really talking about freedom in general and not any specific kind of freedom."

At this point Father Canavan warned of the dangers of reducing, without remainder, religious freedom into religious rights. "Religious freedom may mean many things. But when you're talking about a civil right, you're talking about a legally defined right. And there are limits to what you can do by law, even in the protection of freedom. That's essential to remember. I greatly distrust the civil libertarian mentality that wants to take every ideal and make it into something that can be enforced by the courts. That's just as bad as the suppression of freedom."

Canavan went on to develop an alternative to understanding religious freedom as religious rights. "Given our culture, whenever we start talking about religious freedom, we're talking about rights. We're talking in terms of the individual person and his claims. But we could approach the same question from another angle, through a series of distinctions through which political theory has, for the last 2,500 years, articulated itself. Social forces do determine a lot in history; nonetheless, since we are human beings, we have to arrive at some rational understanding of and reasons for what we're doing.

"Through history we move through distinctions between church and state, between state and society, and between society and the individual. Accordingly, one way of posing the basic question of political theory is to ask, What are the aims, purposes, and goals of the state? What is it there to do? The state isn't the whole of society. It's simply an organization of society that pursues certain goals. You can argue for religious freedom from the viewpoint that the promotion or limitation of religion simply isn't one of the goals that we assign to the thing we call the state.

"Then you join the issue of the human person and his rights by asking, Why are these limitations placed on these powers of the state? That takes us to an understanding of what a human being is. What is the essence of a human person? That's the key question. Notice, however, that the answer to it has to be a public, political, social answer. Any given society, if it is establishing religious freedom or limiting it, is going to give an answer—an answer that is true or false, good or bad, but not simply an individualistic answer—to the key question. If religious freedom is to be effective, we have to come to some conclusion about what we think the essence of the human person is. But this is, of course, a far cry from saying that the essence of a human being is a sovereign will, which is what the liberal tradition tends to do."

Stephen Post then indicated that Canavan's means of posing the problem "is very different from that of the free church tradition. That tradition says that religious liberty is something given by God and that people shouldn't interfere with it because by doing so they're interfering with the freedom of God himself." Post also wondered about bending religious liberty toward agape: "What happens if religious liberty involves certain acts of self-abnegation which are so radical that they would violate any concept of human dignity, needs, rights, and so forth?"

George Weigel then concluded the third session of the conference. "If you ask what sustains democratic commitments, if you ask what sustains commitment to conducting a civil public discourse, the answer is the notion of religious tolerance—that we not kill each other over what constitutes the will of God. As Richard Neuhaus said quite rightly a couple of years ago, what sustains that for most people in America is a belief that it is the will of God that we not kill each other over our disagreements about the will of God. The empirical evidence of that is pretty overwhelming."

CAUTIONARY NOTES ON FREEDOM

The final session of the conference took as its starting point a chapter from Professor Mary Ann Glendon's book entitled *Abortion and Divorce in Western Law* (Harvard University Press, 1987). Introducing her subject, Glendon said, "Let me begin by admitting that I felt a certain amount of apprehension when Richard Neuhaus informed me that my role was to supply the 'cautions' in this conference. The task of expressing anything less than wholehearted enthusiasm for what we all agree is a good thing is not an entirely enviable one. Over the past two days, however, I think I've discerned not only a variety of understandings about what we mean when we speak of political, economic, and religious liberties, but also some reservations about the pursuit of these freedoms to the possible exclusion of other social goods. For my part, I don't want to dissent from the shared assumption that freedoms (leaving aside for a moment the problems of defining them) are rightly assigned a high value in our society. Rather, I want to introduce into our discussion of them what might be called a tragic view.

"My starting point is the simple observation that there have been many shades of meaning in the terms 'freedom' and 'liberty' as we've used them in our discussion. We've spoken of freedom from external coercion, official and unofficial; of freedom from want; of freedoms from and freedoms for; of positive freedoms and negative freedoms. George Weigel has drawn our attention to the importance of interior freedom as constitutive of human personhood. And our diverse religious traditions encourage us to keep in mind the kind of freedom that consists in triumph over pride and passion, emancipation through conquest of the self. These slips and slides of meaning in themselves should put us on guard about a concept like freedom, which has such a powerful hold on our individual and collective imaginations."

Glendon then sketched her five cautionary notes. "My first observation is that it may be prudent to remember that liberties, like other abstract ideals we cherish, can appear in degraded forms. Our languages give us an alternative word to express this: they enable us to speak of how liberty can drift into license, *eleutheria* into *exousia*. A somewhat different but related point is that even when liberties are not especially debased they often have a dark side that should at the very least be examined. A third caution is that liberties, like our other ideals, may exact a price, and that there is an important difference between deciding they're worth the price and pretending that no price exists. A fourth observation, one especially pertinent to this conference, is that liberties frequently involve conflicts, not only between one person's freedoms and another's, or between minorities' and majorities' freedoms, but also between one kind of liberty and another. This is especially true in times, like our own, of proliferating liberties. Finally—and this is a point that relates especially to the United States—many of the meanings that we assign to the concepts of political, economic, and religious liberty are highly individualistic ones. Accordingly, it seems worthwhile to raise the questions of whether and to what extent these American understandings are problematic, and whether there are alternative understandings of freedom that are compatible with democracy.

"The classic statement of the first problem I've raised is found in Plato's *Republic*, where Socrates and Adeimantus are discussing the very subject that has been the center of our attention for the past two days—the relationship between democracy and freedom. Like nearly everyone here, Socrates and his interlocutor start out in substantial agreement that freedom is *the* distinguishing characteristic of democratic cities. Socrates points out that democracies can be observed to be places where a man may say and do what he likes and where an individual is able to order his life as he pleases. It also seems to be characteristic of these places, he says, that we find the greatest variety of human natures there. 'All very true,' says Adeimantus. 'This then,' says Socrates in a memorable passage, 'seems likely to be the fairest of all regimes, being like an embroidered robe which is spangled with every sort of flower.' 'Quite so,' says Adeimantus. Thus encouraged, Socrates goes on to list more of the virtues of these wonderful regimes where freedom is central. There is no compulsion to participate in government—either to rule or to be ruled; or to go to war when others do; or to keep the peace if one does not wish to. 'And,' says Socrates, 'isn't it exquisite how gentle they are toward those who have been adjudged guilty of crimes? Where else would we see such people carrying on as usual in the midst of the city? Furthermore, these cities are not petty or snobbish when it comes to qualifications to rule—they don't care a bit about how a political figure has conducted his life so long as he is well-disposed to the multitude.' At this point, Adeimantus is getting a little nervous—and well he might, for Socrates is about to pose the question of whether the single-minded pursuit of liberty in a polity can somehow paradoxically destroy both democracy and freedom.

"This question—which I bring up not to elaborate but merely to suggest a possible line of discussion—leads to the related matter of what I've called the dark side of our liberties. I think the dark side of freedom is a problem precisely to the degree that liberties are pursued by an individual or a society to the exclusion of other goods. The power of various notions of liberty is such that it can blind us to other values that in many political traditions and most religious traditions would be regarded as liberty's indispensable correlatives. These values include, for example, an awareness of mutual dependence and an active discourse about the common good. (Note that I don't say 'the pursuit of the common good,' which for us moderns is a much more problematic concept, and for heterogeneous

Americans is a practical obstacle of the first order.) In other words, rights, liberties, and freedoms should be seen as having a social dimension. Rights are perhaps better understood as things intertwined with moral and political obligations than as trump cards in the legal games of liberal society. Similarly, a proper understanding of liberty may include the ideas of restraint under law and self-restraint—that is, of what are sometimes called the republican virtues.

"The darkness to which I have alluded, then, is the obverse of liberty, independence, and self-reliance. It is the individual and group egoism, the isolation and alienation, and the neglect of the weak and vulnerable that are fostered by certain understandings of liberty. We Americans, it seems to me, are especially prone to overlook these dangers of overemphasizing individual liberty. One example of this American habit of mind came to my attention as I was reading Jane Jacobs' account of how she became a Canadian citizen. The Canadian naturalization authorities asked Mrs. Jacobs to study a single printed sheet of information about what it means to be a Canadian. The most important thing, the document declared—indeed, 'the chief duty of a Canadian'—is 'to get along well with one's neighbors.' I couldn't help comparing this view of citizenship with the one that was articulated during my daughter's naturalization ceremony in Boston, where she was told, at the age of six, about all the *rights* she would have as an American citizen.

"Another example concerns the peculiar American legal approach to abortion. Our Supreme Court now routinely speaks of a woman's constitutional right to an abortion, a formulation which most Europeans—including those who would be considered pro-choice—would find quite shocking. Indeed, the United States is the only country in the world where abortion is conceptualized in the law as an individual right. Other countries where abortion law is quite liberal typically make it clear that abortion involves the taking of developing human life, and then proceed to consider whether and under what circumstances it should be treated as excusable and therefore exempt from punishment.

"I now proceed to my third caution—that liberties come

at a price. If we conceive of freedom as the absence of restraints imposed by the state, we have to face the well-known disadvantages of leaving the structure and functioning of the social order to be governed by the play of private relations of power. After considering the alternatives, we may decide that the price is worth paying. But it would be a mistake to do so without full awareness that this view of liberty regularly favors the strong. If a free society is also to be a humane society, it must not fail to find a way to respond to the plight of the losers. Furthermore, while it may be a virtue of economic freedom that, as Peter Berger has told us, the economy escapes the control of the state, we should be aware that the state may not escape the control of the economy, that public power and agencies can be captured by powerful private associations and actors. In addition, in modern economies the distinction between state and economy is increasingly tenuous.

"The obvious point to be made about all this, and one to which I wish we had devoted more discussion, is that we need not make either/or choices in the area of economic liberty. All modern liberal democracies in fact have mixed economies. The most important questions in practice thus concern the optimal proportions of the mix between market and regulatory ordering, and the optimal allocation of power among governments, central and local, and intermediate voluntary associations within a given country at a given time.

"So far as conflicts among freedoms are concerned, my comments will be brief because several of these conflicts have already been brought out in our discussions, particularly by Andrew Sullivan's observation that there may be a serious tension between democratic, pluralistic capitalism and religious liberty. Peter Berger responsed to this suggestion by asserting that modernity, rather than capitalism, is the culprit, and that socialism is at least equally in tension with religious liberty. I think that Professor Berger's statements contain a great deal of truth, and yet they seem to pass a little too lightly over the dark side of economic liberty. On this matter, I think Tocqueville's distinction between hard and soft tyranny is helpful. On the modern horizon that we all share, capitalism may have its own distinctive way of undermining religious liberty. That is, a regime founded on the emancipation and legitimation of greed may tend to create a certain kind of citizen whose material preoccupations make it quite difficult for him or her to achieve either religious or political liberty. Thus, while conceding Berger's point that modernity has set the basic conditions, I would nevertheless want us to attend closely to the implications of our own particular form of modernity for the formation of the human personality and for our spiritual and political life.

"My final observation is simply an elaboration of the point that when we Americans use the terms 'liberty' and 'freedom,' we tend to endow them with highly individualistic meanings. In addition to blocking out other social goods, these special understandings of freedom make it extraordinarily difficult for us to achieve a balanced understanding of the importance *for individuals* of mediating structures such as families, neighborhoods, churches, and workers' associations. It is possible that the preservation of all liberty that is not license requires citizens with virtues that can be developed only within such groups. If so, it is a paradox of liberty that it may require attention to the maintenance of associations which are not themselves models of democracy and freedom, groups which may in fact be little hotbeds of inequality and constraints.

"Our American legal system is a museum of examples of the difficulties produced by a concept of a liberty that sees only individuals in their relation to the state. Our Supreme Court has had great difficulty in its First Amendment jurisprudence with the communitarian religions, largely because our bias toward individualism is, in this area, reinforced by an essentially Protestant conception of religion as involving man and God without intermediaries. In similar fashion, the recent history of our labor law has been marked by an increasing failure on the part of official decisionmakers to understand and appreciate the basic concept of solidarity and by their tendency to imagine the workplace as composed of profit-maximizing individual workers. Our legal system seems to lack the conceptual apparatus to grapple with the problem of how to reconcile individual liberties in John Stuart Mill's sense with the liberties of those persons who flourish only within communities and who therefore have a legitimate claim that their communities should not be undermined by the state."

"Marvelous!" said Neuhaus in response. "Obviously, we have our work cut out for us this afternoon."

American Individualism, Closely Considered

Raymond Gastil was the first to take issue with Glendon. "Professor Glendon's comparison of the United States and European countries, of American individualism and the European situation, bothers me. There are a lot of characteristics of American society that aren't so individualistic. In the nineteenth century Tocqueville characterized American society as being a society of joiners, of people who belong to a wide variety of organizations. And today, for example, Americans are more likely to join churches than Europeans are. Again, while the cautions are worthwhile, I'm not sure that there's such a big gap between American society and European societies or that there's anything very special about the American commitment to individualism."

"One might suggest that the individualism Professor Glendon criticizes is out of synch with the American reality, which is more attuned to a communal form of life," Neuhaus urged.

Then Glendon answered Gastil: "The differences between the United States and western Europe aren't big differences but are matters of nuance. The differences are really slight, but the spirit of the differences penetrates every detail of the legal systems. American society and western European societies are all individualistic, but our legal system is much more individualistic than the western European systems. In our legal documents, for example, we don't habitually couple rights with responsibilities."

Criticism of individualism is often a veiled criticism of capitalism. Aware of this, Peter Berger noted two important criticisms of capitalism. "One, and the most obvious one, is the symbolic power of the market. This is what Marx had in mind when he noted that in capitalism everything—all values and even the person himself—could come to be regarded as a marketable commodity. That's a dark side of capitalism, one that penetrates American thought and language. We express so much in marketing terms: 'Let me sell this to you,' 'I won't buy this,' 'What's the bottom line?' 'There's no money in this idea,' and so on."

"Even the use of the term 'values' is suspect," added Neuhaus.

"Possibly," said Berger. Then he continued, "I think we would all agree that that's an unfortunate kind of symbolic universe.

"The other criticism of capitalism is less obvious but is probably just as important. It concerns that aspect of capitalism which Schumpeter called its 'creative destruction,' which means that everything that is new is better. In capitalism there is a built-in obsoleteness of things which can then translate into the obsoleteness of values, of persons, and so on. Friendships are freely exchanged. Nothing lasts, because what's new is always better. Again, I think we would agree that this is a feature of American life which, so far as one might trace it to capitalism, represents an unfortunate aspect of capitalism."

"Once one has made those concessions," Berger went on, "one has to make this point: For most people the features of a capitalist worldview, as they intrude into their everyday lives and thoughts, are not all-governing. There are other things going on at the same time. The person who thinks of himself, of his family, and of his values in exclusively market terms is unique. In fact, most of us would regard this person as a rather pathological case. Among the other things that have significance, the two most important are family and religion, which prevent one from looking at the world only in market terms. To live in any modern society always is to live in a kind of active, complicated schizophrenia. That's what pluralism means: you participate in differents things that involve different habits, different symbols, and so on. This is also true of capitalism. A businessman goes home and goes to church and dabbles in hobbies and other activities. So, there is a multiplicity not only of other values but also of other institutions that embody those values."

Glendon then clarified her position: "My idea of the soft threat, however, has to do with a preoccupation with comfort and material security that makes it difficult to have an interior life. This is something that was discussed a few thousand years ago."

"Exactly," Berger responded. "It isn't capitalism. It isn't specifically capitalism."

"But capitalism generalized the pursuit of comfort throughout entire societies," claimed Paul Stallsworth.

George Weigel then added a new wrinkle to the issue of whether capitalism's individualism is good or bad for people. "Let's take on the Yuppie problem, the BMW syndrome, for a moment. Couldn't one argue that in societies with subsistence economies, people are scrambling day in and day out simply to be fed, clothed, and sheltered? In such societies there appears to be less social space. One of the paradoxes of the market is precisely its fecundity; if taken proper advantage of, it creates the social space for pursuit of what we would all regard as higher goods."

"That's an empirical issue," Glendon commented.

Berger followed with a defense of capitalism: "Critics of capitalism, including the current pope, continually point to materialism and greed. But those are precisely two things that can't be ascribed to capitalism. I don't see that capitalism is any more materialistic than any other economic system. And greed, I'm sure, is a universal human characteristic. So if we're looking at the cautions that Mary Ann Glendon correctly points to, we have to look at causes other than capitalism."

"Greed may be universal," replied Neuhaus, "but can't one argue that certain systems encourage it and are based upon it more than others?"

Berger responded: "What's specifically capitalistic about my wanting to have a lot of things? In fact, since capitalism makes the accumulation of things easier, one might therefore argue that the passion of greed becomes less dangerous."

"Perhaps," Jim Finn interjected. "But there is an element in capitalism that goes in a different direction. Of course greed isn't new. You can find it through all societies. What is new is that in a capitalistic society greed has more to operate on. The critical mass that greed operates on is very different in a capitalist society. For example, when I check the back page of the *New York Times*, an ad proclaims, 'Nowhere in the world will you be able to get a better view of Central Park than in this high-rise building on Park Avenue for X dollars'—a huge sum of money. Such a statement, silly though it is, encourages greed. It encourages greed in a way that wasn't possible before capitalism entered world history. If greed is inflamed in a virulent way throughout society, then it takes away the energy that might otherwise go into other activities and that in the past did go into other activities, including things related to the common good and to interior space."

Weigel spoke up at this point. "My favorite example is the unbelievable Merrill Lynch slogan: 'To Know No Boundaries.' If that's the moral lesson of capitalism, then there's a problem. On the other hand, why should we expect the economic system to cope with that problem by itself? I think of Michael Novak's triad for society—the economic system, the moral-cultural system, and the political system. Through the moral-cultural system and the political system we have some capacity to shape, temper, and fundamentally challenge the kinds of notions that are generated by some parts of the market."

Now Frithjof Bergmann joined in, venturing a scenario illustrating how capitalism gave rise to a destructive form of individualism. "There's a factual point that is crucial. Among anthropologists it is old hat that, contrary to what many people assume, all early cultures were not cultures in which people struggled and worked around the clock in order to survive. Amazingly enough, it has been shown that in pre-modern cultures people worked only two hours a day. All of these early cultures were very leisurely cultures, very comfortable cultures, in which people had time to do any number of things besides work or struggle for income or struggle for survival.

"Remember that Max Weber says that of course capitalism wasn't motivated by greed. Greed is universal. What got capitalism started was Calvinism, because Calvinism tied the matter of material success to grace and to being one of the elect. If you succeeded in material pursuits, that showed the world that God loved you. If you didn't succeed, that showed you were damned. It took religion to get capitalism going.

"Weber also points out that capitalism resulted in the dissolution of traditional cultures. It turned life into an individual struggle. Most people who previously had lived very comfortable peasant lives found that in a capitalistic system they had to hire themselves out as wage labor to survive. That's something of the history of how we got to a state of such rampant individualism. Capitalism creates a society in which individuals struggle for survival, which wasn't previously the case. That struggle for survival fosters an individualism that becomes rampant and boundless and threatening."

Raymond Gastil's account of the history of work differed from Bergmann's: "The anthropological story is that a primitive society, a pre-agricultural society, had extremely short work hours. Bushmen, for example, worked fifteen hours a week. But after the agricultural revolution, people started working much longer and much harder than that."

George Weigel noted that "sixty years ago in this country we had sixty-hour workweeks. Now we have forty-hour work-weeks. So it's crazy to say that somehow there's been this exponential, continuous increase in the time spent working."

"No," retorted Bergmann. "It's just that we went crazy under capitalism and started working sixty hours a week. But now we're regaining our sanity somewhat by cutting back to forty hours a week."

Freedoms Threatened

Taking on a new subject, Kent Hill spoke about the survivability of democracy. "We have talked too little about duty and responsibility. It strikes me that this factor—let's call it the moral character of citizens in a democracy—is so critically important that we should deal with it as a separate factor. The fact that a society allows religious freedom doesn't necessarily mean that it will exercise that freedom in a way which will produce the kind of moral virtues that are necessary for democracy to survive.

"If we understand individualism in the extreme to mean selfishness, and if we understand selfishness to be a factor that undermines both community and the possibility of the democratic experiment, then I would like to advance three propositions. Be warned: I'm deliberately trying to be a bit provocative here. The three propositions go something like this. First, democracy cannot survive apart from the presence of responsible citizenship, and such responsible citizenship requires the ability and the willingness to place the good of the whole above narrow individual interests. Second, religion is a major—though not the sole—support for the virtues that underlie responsible citizenship. And third, an increasingly secular society will not be a conducive environment for the democratic experiment. All of this says that you could conceivably have religious, political, and economic freedom and survive for a time, but that state wouldn't continue for very long unless the critical factor of moral character in the citizenry reappears."

Conferees had singled out excessive individualism as one threat to freedom, and Hill identified immoral or amoral citizenry as a second threat. Now Stephen Post added a third: "Forgetting that freedom is a gift from God is a great threat to freedom. I agree with Thomas Jefferson on that point—that freedom is essentially a divine gift and that we should use it in proper moral and covenantal fashion. Saint Paul—who said, 'Where the Spirit of the Lord is, there is liberty'—was a favorite of the preachers prior to the American Revolution in New England. Those theological themes are very important. Somehow human freedom is part of the body of Judeo-Christian theology, and without that foundation we probably can't sustain freedom as well as we think we can."

Later in the discussion Post confided, "Frankly, I'm a little surprised that we haven't theologized more in this discussion. I confess that I'm something of an Actonian. Lord Acton wrote ten thousand pages of notes on the theology of freedom. They were never published, which is too bad—they're full of wonderful aphorisms. For example, 'God so loved freedom that he even permitted sin,' which is a play on John 3:16. As a nineteenth-century Catholic liberal, Acton saw a certain resonance and connection between Christian ideas and the preservation of human freedom. Maybe in order to sustain freedom in this nation we need to reconstruct the theological premise of freedom that the Deists had. The Puritans also had it: many of them proclaimed along with Saint Paul that freedom isn't something that we can take or leave; rather, it's something we must accept because it is given by the divine. I wonder if

freedom can be sustained if a society avoids the kind of theological framework that at least believers think is essential to
freedom."

"That's especially important because the majority of
Americans describe themselves as more or less religious,"
Neuhaus added. "But the genuinely new thing has been the
effort of the cultural elites and the knowledge class of this
society over the last half century to try to formulate what never
would have occurred to Jefferson or Rousseau or Locke—to try
to sustain the democratic procedure without some kind of
moral and, at least for democratic and popular purposes, religiously grounded legitimation. This has really been an aston-
ishing experiment in which the courts have most recklessly
been leading the way. So, what several of us around this table
are proposing is not a new thing. What we're proposing is that
we stop the rather suicidal experiment in which we've been
engaged for the last several decades."

Father Canavan described a fourth threat to freedom.
"The language of individualism does drive out other forms of
discourse," he began. "This doesn't happen all the time, but it
does happen a great deal. If you were to ask a student in one
of my classes a question about something rather simple—for
instance, 'Do you think cannibalism is wrong?'—the answer
you would get from a class that is 75 percent Roman Catholic
is, 'Well, having been raised as I was, with my system of values,
I wouldn't like it.' None of the students will say that cannibalism is simply wrong. Why? Because of the dominant language
of individualism.

"Also, when you read the newspapers, you notice the
frequency with which this country seems unable to deal with
a single issue until it's reduced to a conflict of rights. Abortion
is the primary example: there we have the rights of the mother
pitted against the rights of the fetus. That isn't the only way of
thinking about the issue. But apparently the American mind is
basically unable to think about issues unless they're understood as conflicts of rights.

"In our society the limits on the power of the state are
based on the rights of the individual. According to Stanley
Hauerwas, this undermines mediating structures, because such

structures are then understood as nothing but *voluntary* associations created by individual wills. We root so much in the rights of the individual that in court cases involving an individual and a nonpublic institution, the individual prevails.

"This sounds like Chicken Little saying that the sky is falling. Well, I don't think the sky is falling, but I do think that it's collapsing slowly or crumbling at the edges or deteriorating.

"In *Statecraft as Soulcraft*," Canavan concluded, "George Will remarks that liberalism has given us government which believes in the moral equality of appetites. That's one of those sweeping journalistic remarks, but there's enough truth in it to warrant attention. If you ask, 'Where does democracy undermine freedom?' I think the threat is precisely there—in the subjectivization of the whole idea of the good. That makes the notion of a public morality impossible. In the Georgia sodomy law case, U.S. Supreme Court Justice Blackmun wrote a hymn of praise to the right of the individual to determine his conception of the good, unregulated by any conception of public morality. This points to a profound split in thinking in the legal profession and to a very powerful current of thought in our jurisprudence which is saying in effect that liberty is the moral equality of appetites. That, it seems to me, is where the idea of freedom is most menaced right now. Other people could read the same set of documents and come to a much more sanguine conclusion. But that's how I feel about it."

"Thank you, Frank," Neuhaus responded. "But there's a touch of irony here. You ended on the note with which your students begin, by qualifying your statement with 'That's *my* reading of the situation' or 'That's *my* feeling.' "

Rights against/or/and Goods

Before embarking on a discussion of individual rights and collective goods, the group listened as Martin Golding discussed lawmaking. "One of the essential characteristics of modern legal theory is the notion that somebody can come in and legally restructure everything without any attention to what came before. The actual making of law is a revolutionary idea. In the United States, which has a fluid, changing society, lawmaking has little sense of tradition."

"Both in continental Europe and in the Anglo-American tradition the idea of law as command is the dominant idea," Glendon observed.

"As distinct from law as what?" Neuhaus asked.

"As distinct from law as coming from the bottom up—that is, law as custom elaborated over the ages," Mary Ann Glendon replied. "That's the idea of English common law. There's also the practical notion of law as a way of educating citizens to be noble and wise and directed toward the common good. These notions are tossed aside by the modern project, which has to do with made law, with law coming from the top down. All of us are involved in that modern project. But what has significant practical consequences for our problems today in the continental and American legal systems is that the continentals kept alive as undercurrents some fragments of the old classical notion of law and the customary notion of law. That saved them, in a way, on the issues of divorce, abortion, and dependency. In addition, on the Continent the whole range of issues having to do with surrogate motherhood, the human body in commerce, experimentation on fetuses, and genetic engineering seems to be treated within a legal framework that depends on some of the older traditions."

Now the stage was set for Professor Glendon to initiate a lengthy discussion of individual rights and collective goods. "Is rights language the only way to talk about abortion?" Glendon began. "No, it's a very peculiar, American way to talk about abortion. To see how peculiar it is, consider West Germany. In West Germany the constitution, unlike our constitution, has the following: a provision establishing the equality of the sexes, a provision establishing a right to life, and a provision establishing what we would call a right to privacy but what they call the right to the free unfolding of the personality. These three rights are in tension with each other, and each in some way bears on the abortion question. What do the West German constitutional courts do with that? They refuse to discuss abortion in terms of rights. Instead they say, 'What we're dealing with here is a question of goods, social goods, and in our constitution there is a hierarchy of goods. Because of our recent history, the highest place in that hierarchy is accorded to life, not as a right but as a good to which the whole society is dedicated.' This way of thinking and speaking helps them to avoid the kind of flat either/or decision that rights language always gets us involved in, because in rights language there is no compromise.

"The road to wisdom on the abortion issue involves saying that a number of goods are involved. One certainly is the good of life. Another has to do with compassion for women in extremely lonely and frightening situations. And maybe it's best to do what the West Germans do—to protect the good of human life by attending to women's needs for social support. Maybe the state has an affirmative obligation to provide financial and other kinds of assistance to pregnant women. Most importantly, the resolution of this issue should be left to the legislatures, which means that the matter isn't closed once and for all and that discourse about the problem can continue. Education, bargaining, and persuasion can take place, and the society can develop an approach.

"U.S. Supreme Court decisions on privacy define privacy as the right to be left alone. That formulation is enormously significant. It should be contrasted with the West German idea of the right to the free unfolding of the personality; at least that notion is open to a social dimension."

"Look," Andrew Sullivan interjected, "people who are arguing in favor of rights aren't doing so out of some abstract preference for rights over goods. They're doing so fundamentally because they accept the fact that there is no consensus on the good. Rights language is a product of the radical fragmentation of common moral understandings in the West. At certain times and in certain places—in the case of Germany, for example—there is a massive historical experience that overtakes or swamps the moral fragmentation. But that isn't the case in the United States today. Given that, we have to use the language of rights.

"There is the argument that goes like this: If we have only a language of rights, then paradoxically we will not be able to sustain those rights because the common good or the moral virtue necessary to sustain them will be lacking. I've never really bought that argument. As long as there is a profound common understanding of the prior inviolability of rights upheld by the Constitution, then I don't see any inherent instability in that construction. It seems to generate its own common good, which is that there shall be no common good. The procedure, then, becomes the substance. When we look around us in America, it appears that this is what Americans really believe. Liberalism's attack on the common good and on moral virtue has succeeded and may actually be coherent."

Neuhaus quizzed Sullivan on his position: "Are you prepared to say that if a society can get by without any moral legitimation of its procedures, then the question of why people must obey the procedures and the laws simply isn't going to arise?"

"The question does arise," Sullivan responded, "and it's answered by the claim that there should never be this big, contentious argument about the common good. That's the great, binding factor in our democracy. That's the great moral cohesion."

"That's the empty shrine," Ken Myers added.

"That's a provocative statement, Andrew," commented Neuhaus, "but then you warned us that it would be."

Next Peter Berger entered the discussion. "The point that Andrew raises is crucial to this discussion. I totally agree with him when he says that the language of rights isn't due to some strange metaphysical mistake but that it's necessary because it isn't possible for society to agree on what the good is.

"I was a little troubled by Mary Ann Glendon's example of the West German constitutional court. She referred to it as if it were an enormous repository of wisdom. Maybe it is—I'm not familiar with it. But I'm nervous about this because behind it is the notion that the court knows what the common good is, and I'm profoundly suspicious of that notion. I don't trust that court any more than I trust anyone else."

To this Glendon replied, "I share your concern about the West German constitutional court defining the good. But as I see it, that court compares very favorably with our own high court. The German court finds sources of the good in constitutional language and in legislation. It doesn't invent the good."

Berger responded with a pertinent anecdote. "Let me try to sharpen my point with a story. The British once occupied the Sind in India, which is now part of Pakistan. The British imposed what they always did, minimal British law, leaving everything else as it was. They did prohibit the burning of widows, which was customary in the Sind. Subsequently, a Brahmanic delegation came to see a British general, who told them that they couldn't burn their widows. The delegation said that they couldn't be prohibited from burning their widows because it was an ancient tradition of their people. Without a moment's hesitation the general replied, 'It is an ancient tradition of my people that we hang men who burn women alive. Let us all follow our traditions.'

"Why am I mentioning this story? Because a major question that pertains to discussions like this one is, How can one achieve in American public life something like the assurance of the British general in the story? While I have enormous sympathy for that question, I'm also skeptical of it.

"I think it's important to continue discussing the matter," Berger went on. "Nevertheless, I remain skeptical. The project of constructing or reconstructing an American public philosophy is one that I'm not sure is possible to achieve. I regret this. I'd be very happy if it were possible. If this can't happen globally, maybe it can happen in certain areas—on the issues of abortion or human rights in Iran or whatever. But an overall agreement on the good—I doubt very much that that's possible."

Neuhaus then gave his opinion of Sullivan's statement. "I don't disagree with Andrew about the commitment to, the allegiance to, the sense of duty to democratic procedure and to the open-ended character of the procedure. But there are two things I would add that Andrew didn't add but perhaps wouldn't object to. First, this commitment is informed by a Christian and essentially an eschatological understanding of history. That's a point of tenuous convergence between the notion of democratic process and a Christian understanding of history. Second, what is the procedure? The procedure is the serious deliberation, carried on through various ways and means, on the good and the common good."

Glendon followed with a comment. "Yes, Andrew's assertion about why we talk about rights is correct. And maybe there is no escape from it. But it's important to keep in mind that this rights talk is a human invention and a rather modern invention. It has swept across the world—even the Vatican uses it now. My suggestion is that if we're going to use the language, we should remember that it's artificial and that for a religious person it is certainly strange. A religious person, when first confronted with the idea of rights, would have to say, 'Well, we don't really have the right to anything, and our existence is radically contingent. Everything hangs by a thread.' We can grow up with a language of rights, which enables us to live together in a heterogeneous society, but we need to worry about using rights language as a rhetorical intensifier. We also have to worry about the proliferation of rights; our Supreme Court multiplies them with great virtuosity. As with all powerful concepts, we have to be aware of the power of rights language and its dangers."

At this juncture David Novak worried aloud about whether or not a society organized only on the basis of rights could survive. "The current project of the American republic—the total bifurcation of life into private good and public necessity—is intolerable for the person seeking some kind of unity in life. That's Plato. We should also take note of Churchill. In his reflections on what led up to World War II, he indicated that he felt that the attitude fostered by British philosophy had led to a moral breakdown, an inability to face Nazism. Part of this was the 1932 resolution of the Oxford Union, the debating society, a resolution proposed by a moral philosopher. It went this way: 'Resolved: I will not die for king and country.' That's an incoherent declaration, because if society is to protect one's private good, society has to be able to marshal defenses against its enemies, and society cannot operate against its enemies if they know that nobody is willing to die for that society. It's like the argument on nuclear deterrence: If my private moral purity leads to the opposite result of what I want, then there's something wrong with my private moral purity. Therefore, the idea of right being a private good that has a binding claim on the public ultimately becomes incoherent because society, which is supposed to protect that good, cannot survive that kind of philosophy."

Contesting the Common Good

Raymond Gastil tried to qualify the attraction of a common, public good by which a society might order its life. "As a youth

I studied the evolution of Nazi law from the 1920s through the 1930s. In that study I was struck by the terminology of 'duty.' The emphasis was not so much on rights as it was on the specified duties of citizens. For example, an individual who saw someone fall into the water had a duty to rescue that victim; if the individual didn't perform his duty, he was punished. This kind of language can sound very attractive, but it wasn't so attractive in some of the ways it worked out."

Neuhaus quickly questioned Gastil: "Aren't you skewing the question by putting common-good countries, so to speak, only in the camp of unfree societies? In the case of Nazi Germany, the common good wasn't arrived at freely and democratically."

"But it was using the same kind of language," Gastil claimed.

"But there the *state* was defining the common good and inventing the language," George Weigel put in.

Then Mary Ann Glendon mediated: "In an audience like this I didn't think it was necessary to say that there are dangers involved in the concept of the common good, just as there are dangers involved in the concept of individualism. We Americans are all too familiar with the dark side of regimes that we don't participate in, but we tend to blind ourselves to the dark side of some of our own most cherished ideals. So I'm not holding any brief for the common good as a replacement for ideas of individualism. I think the trick here is to find the optimal mixes, corrections, and balances in liberties and rights—religious, political, and economic."

By pointing to one of the disadvantages of the theory and practice of rights, Martin Golding defended the concept of the common good. "Rights language is so absolute," he said. "Consequently, in a conflict formulated as a conflict of rights, one party has to lose. At least that's the way it works in the United States. It's a kind of zero-sum conflict resolution. Either my rights are upheld or your rights are upheld, but somebody has to lose. There are other forms of dispute settlement that don't use the language of rights. For example, in the process of mediation, labor mediators often point out that in order to mediate a dispute, the first thing that has to be done is to get the parties to stop talking about their rights. As long as they stand on and insist on their rights, mediation is impossible."

Glendon then observed, "One of the mysteries of American law is how a thinker such as John Stuart Mill exerted such enormous influence on the American legal system. We got a straight shot of Mill—a sort of simplified, vulgarized Mill—in our U.S. Supreme Court decisions. That, to a great extent, explains why our constitutional jurisprudence looks the way it does."

"I like that—mainlining Mill," noted Neuhaus. "That explains a great deal of what's gone wrong in American law."

Responding to Golding's point about winning all the chips or losing all the chips in the legal arena, Glendon continued, "There's a problem with democratic institutions. One of the ways in which our society is special is in the relationship between court and legislature, as they have evolved. As our Supreme Court increasingly undertakes decisionmaking about the basic directions of society, it not only gets involved in absolute winning and absolute losing, which isn't characteristic of the more compromising legislative process, but it also causes the legislative process to atrophy and become the object of contempt. If we want to imagine a way in which our institutions could mediate, and a way in which pluralism could be accommodated, and a way in which there wouldn't always be an absolute winner and an absolute loser, then we have some thinking to do about the legislature as a place where bargaining, education, and persuasion could take place.

"The dialogue on the common good could go on in the legislative branch. But the Court has made it easy for legislators not to do what they're supposed to do. Legislators don't like to take firm stands on controversial issues, so it's been wonderful for them for the Court to take issues like abortion off their hands."

"But that's democratically dangerous," asserted Weigel.

Veering away from legal-legislative issues, Michael Warder took a different tack on the common good. "Affirming the good is good. It needs to be done. But we might also think about the bad, not to mention the ugly. If we think of evils or things to be avoided, we might find some agreements. Part of the problem is that in the name of the good—even in the name of religion—so much bad has been done. And people are afraid of that. So, if positing the idea of the good, especially the religious good, is frightening to some, then it might be helpful instead to talk in terms of bad things, or unfair things, or unjust things. We can, I think, readily agree about those things. And it really doesn't harm anybody."

Golding's earlier comment on legal winning and losing triggered a comment from Neuhaus. "Take, once again, the example of the ten people on the island. When the process is vindicated and the minority doesn't prevail, they nevertheless prevailed in the sense that they participated in the vindication of the process. They were confident that they wouldn't be excluded from the continuing contestation that the process provides for and makes possible.

"Let me be very practical for a moment. In American public life today we have something that's worthy of being called a crisis. With the emergence of the Religious New Right, we have a very large number of Americans, millions upon millions, who are engaged in all kinds of rather aggressive incursions into the public square but who are very uncommitted, for the most part, to the procedure. Why? Because they've seen the ways in which the procedure has been used, in the name of simply following and advancing the procedure, to in fact impose a very substantive definition of the good. Again, with disturbing frequency, the Dworkins and the Lears and the ACLUs of the world have imposed their notions of the good at the same time they've been saying, 'We can't talk about the good.' That's why everybody has to come out of the closet, so to speak, with respect to the good, and then honestly address the procedure that will never achieve any single party's definition of the good in an entirely satisfactory manner. But if we're to prevent the situation that MacIntyre calls 'politics being civil war carried on by other means,' every party should recognize its commitment to the onging deliberation and the contestation of getting as much of its definition of the common good as it can. Every party should do this while anticipating and accepting in advance the unsatisfactory character of the results, because the procedure at least permits the party's continued participation. I don't think we have that now. And I don't think we can get it unless people become more candid about their statements about the good."

Francis Canavan agreed with Neuhaus: "The appeal to government neutrality in a pluralistic society is flimflam. All it means in practice is that the most relativistic, individualistic, subjectivistic view is the one that wins out and gets established by law. That may be good, but neutral it is not. It can't be. For better or for worse, societies confront moral questions to which they must give some public answers. And their answers won't be neutral.

"The fear seems to be that if we ever admitted that there is such a thing as the common good, it would be some sort of straitjacket forced on society. I don't think that's true. The common good isn't a Platonic idea with fixed, necessary, and eternal content. I like what Michael Walzer says about welfare in *Spheres of Justice*. He makes the point that we shouldn't define welfare in the narrow sense as Aid to Families with Dependent Children. When we talk about welfare, he says, we're not talking about individual rights. Instead, we're really appealing to our conception of the kind of community that we are. That's perfectly and obviously true in American society. Welfare concerns the story we tell about ourselves. For example, we're not the kind of community that allows people to die of hunger. We have homeless people, almost outside the door of the Union League Club, but it bothers us that they're homeless. So we have to ask ourselves what conception we have of ourselves as an organized community, and that means we have an ongoing debate. Translated, the debate hinges on these questions: What is our conception of the common good? What do we as a community owe to each and to all of our members? I see nothing hostile to freedom in that, because we might conceive of freedom as a basic human need. That's not the unlimited freedom of every individual to do whatever he pleases, but the freedom that human beings need to flourish as human beings in what we consider to be a good community."

Neuhaus then responded, "You've said that freedom is a part of the common good. If we take the current Kulturkampf in American society, the People for the American Way and the

Liberty Federation both believe that freedom and the common good are antithetical. One has an understanding of freedom; the other has an understanding of the common good. People for the American Way don't understand that the institutions and procedures of freedom can be protected only by some understanding of the common good. But in fact that can be true only if those who have a notion of the common good believe that freedom is required as an essential component of the common good. The two parties are at war because neither believes that the other understands that its commitment belongs in the package of commitments of the opposing party.

"The People for the American Way have a very definite notion of the common good, but they refuse to come out of the closet with it. They persistently claim that they're dealing only with the procedure. This stokes the fury of the Religious Right and its polemic against secular humanism. And the Religious Right, however crudely it puts its objection, is correct: The other side is dishonest in that people who are always talking rights and procedural language in fact have a very definite notion about what the good society is and how they're going to use the procedure to bring about the good society, regardless of what the majority of the people want."

Relativism as a Common Good?

Andrew Sullivan amused the group as he introduced the conference's last major topic. "I speak as one representing the elite that's driving America to suicide," Sullivan kidded. "Seriously, though, I agree and sympathize enormously with what Pastor Neuhaus has just said. On many occasions I've said similar things.

"But the question is whether society's contemporary inability to agree on a notion of the common good points to some radical disagreement even about essentials. This might signal that the crisis in moral and philosophic cohesion is greater than the old-style differences about what the common good might be. In other words, the crisis—which is the fundamental, radical, moral incoherence that questions even the existence of morality—might be deeper today. If that's the case, then saying

'There has to be a common good, so let's debate it and assume that the procedure is the common good' isn't up to the level of the crisis.

"But the need for a common good still exists. What more honest and sophisticated people who try to think this through might say is that relativism itself performs the function of a common good. Well, you might say that America really isn't like that, and that this common good is really an elite's ideological abstraction that's put upon people who still have religious beliefs. But relativism might be taken as true by this certain group of people. And all of us must admit that relativism is not simply the complete lack of thought, though that temptation is there.

Take the question about cannibalism that Father Canavan posed. In some quarters, the person who refused to pass judgment on cannibalism would be credited with great moral quality. Within that framework we can construct a common good. Building on Father Canavan's example of the Georgia sodomy law case, we can say that we don't care whether people are sodomizing each other, and we feel we have a moral obligation not to care. And we might even want to argue publicly that other people shouldn't care.

"Now, there are real problems with relativism as the common good. One of them, as David Novak pointed out, is national defense: How can a society that has relativism as its common good stand up and defeat Nazism? It's possible that people could be persuaded to defend a private pursuit of whatever they like if they're quite attached to it. For example, 200,000 people marched on Washington to protect their right to do whatever they like in the bedroom. They were quite ferocious about it."

Father Canavan responded: "It's really a Kantian notion that, among people who can't know objective good, the common good consists simply in an ordering and structuring of rights by which we keep out of one another's way in pursuit of private conceptions of the good. I think that's a pseudo-common good. It's not a real common good, because it assumes that nothing is held in common except the agreement to allow everyone to pursue his own good in his own way. As is often pointed out, this seems to work fairly well. We're getting along with it.

"But the danger I see there is that the more the democratic political process becomes simply a contest among interest groups, who have been told that there's no such thing as the common good of justice, the more the process becomes strained. And, needless to say, it can break down under the strain. Furthermore, it can lose its moral legitimacy, because people have been persuaded that there are no common interests and that all we have in common is a set of procedures for resolving conflicts among private interests. I would worry about this if economic growth slacked off—or if we experienced scarcity. For years we've been willing to accept what everybody believes is an unequal and unjust division of the pie because the pie was in fact getting bigger all the time. The system, in that sense, worked. But would it continue to work if the only common bonds were enlightened self-interest and the belief that the pursuit of self-interest is sufficient reason for adhering to the procedures, and if in fact the pie were getting smaller?"

"The relative structure does have a certain amount of emotional pull," replied Sullivan. "So, for example, if you participate in the gay-lesbian march on Washington, you may want to say that in order to preserve the system you have to tighten up economically, even through scarcity, because you value your community. The affective loyalty to the system might develop enough so that it could sustain the system through rough times."

Neuhaus spoke next: "Let's take the abortion issue. Decisions are made about abortion that are clearly consequential and that most of us would be inclined to say are inescapably moral. It has been decided that a very large class of what is unquestionably, from the scientific viewpoint, human life is not to be protected by the community. That's an answer that has been given by the courts—not by the people, not by the legislature—with respect to what kind of community we are. *Roe v. Wade* is one kind of answer to what kind of community we are.

We know what the consequences of this decision are for the aged. Take Dan Callahan's *Setting Limits.* That's not just a proposal. What he writes about is going on now—food and fluids are being withheld from thousands of Americans who are very much at the edge of the law. But the law will catch up to legitimate that practice very quickly. And what about the ripple effect with regard to the handicapped, assisted suicide, euthanasia in many forms, and the black, urban underclass? This has been a development of the last decade, and only in the last few years have people become aware of it. In the context of relativism, where is an effective agent in the society equipped—whether in the legislature or in the courts or in some mediating structure—to say, 'No, you can't do this. You can't extend the logic of *Roe v. Wade* to say these other categories are excluded from the community'?"

"Here is the United States, a country with millions of Christians who are tolerating widespread abortion," Sullivan reminded the group. "Not all of them are. But the fact that the opposition to abortion is not of fantastic, burning intensity speaks loudly."

"But the courts stand in the way of even fantastic, burning opposition having any social effect," Neuhaus reasoned.

Sullivan answered, "But even among Christians in this day and age there is an adherence to relativism that has tempered their opposition to *Roe v. Wade*. Thirty years ago would it have been possible to contemplate this many practicing Christians acquiescing to the present levels of abortion? I think then it would have been quite difficult."

"I readily agree with you on that. And that has to do with decadence in the churches and the loss of a sense of transcendence and authentic religion," Neuhaus argued.

Now Kent Hill joined the discussion. "It's not just a matter of the Christian community *acquiescing* on the abortion issue. It's also a matter of groups in the Christian community actively *supporting* the pro-choice forces. We have hundreds of thousands of dollars going from denominational budgets into the pro-choice lobby, especially the Religious Coalition for Abortion Rights. I even saw a statistic from a major denomination which indicated that the percentage who supported choice within that denomination is higher than the pro-choice percentage in society as a whole.

"Even in the evangelical world, which is the world I'm from, I see this creeping in, not so much in terms of support for choice as in an unwillingness to oppose it. The reason is that people are desperately afraid of being identified with the Right. Apparently there's nothing worse than being identified with the Right, politically or religiously. There seems to be an incredible lack of moral courage.

"In 1985 the senior class of the university at which I taught asked me to give the baccalaureate address. Prior to that I had been thinking about these issues for several months, and I had been struck by this lack of courage. So I felt a strong conviction that I ought to speak on abortion at the baccalaureate ceremony. I went through the wrenching experience of having to decide whether or not to do something like that, knowing what the consequences would be. I went ahead and did it, so I know how painful it can be. I think that that dilemma represents for us in the Christian world a tremendous lack of moral courage. It's a very serious problem."

Peter Berger spoke next. "Father Canavan indicated that at present our society seems to be getting along quite well under relativism. And that's true, despite the abortion issue and so on. But if I may put the point brutally, fetuses don't vote, and neither do people on life-support systems. So apparently the society can get along quite well while disregarding the claims of those who don't have the power to influence what most people do.

"Our society might be headed toward economic decline. One interesting author to look at on this subject is Mancur Olson, who has written *The Rise and Decline of Nations.* He uses the phrase 'distributional coalitions.' What does this rights language translate into in economic terms? It means that our society is an entitlement society. That means the society has many coalitions of people who are interested only in how to distribute goods, not in how to produce them. Olson shows persuasively that the growth of this kind of political phenomenon leads to economic decline or at the very least diminishes economic growth."

Trying to clarify the discussion, Raymond Gastil inquired, "Couldn't relativism be used as an excuse for what really is a clash of different conceptions of the good? In other words, the people putting thousands of dollars behind pro-choice lobbying aren't doing that for the sake of relativism. They're doing it because they have some definition of the good that's different from the pro-life definition."

Neuhaus then entered and ended the discussion. "I agree. The people on the pro-choice side who identify themselves with a dominantly, if not exclusively, procedural definition of the political process do in fact have an understanding of the good. And they want to impose that on the whole society. Again, I would argue that we should clear the air and have a royal fight—because that's what democracy's about: it's a very raucous process, and it should be—beginning with everybody putting their notion of the good on the table. We should acknowledge that there's no way for a society like this one to be sustained without the acknowledgment that a democratic deliberation about differing descriptions of the good is essential.

"Aristotle said that politics is, first of all, an extension of ethics. Second, it functions as an answer to the question, How ought we to order our life together? Politics, then, is about deliberation over this question. It seems to me that the Religious Right and the Right generally—though not libertarians—have the better part of the argument, because at least they're responding to Aristotle's question."

Society, several conferees were suggesting, cannot live by rights alone. Somewhere, somehow, notions of the common good must and will come into play in democratic society. It is best for society, for the mediating institutions of society, and for the members of society for different ideas of the common good to be engaged with honesty, deliberateness, and civility in the public arena. Freedom is both a condition of that deliberation and a likely result of it. This freedom may be partly but is not solely a rights-regarding freedom. This freedom is a freedom with purpose. It is a freedom not devoid of the good, or goods.

Thus, through the two days of our discussion, many of the causes and correlations of freedoms—religious, political, and economic—were pinpointed and generalized, examined and assumed, agreed upon and debated. But finally, it seems, the conference decided, with the able assistance of Mary Ann Glendon, that Aristotle's question—How ought we to order our life together?—is inevitably the question which is ever before society. But Aristotle's question remains forever a question. It is the responsibility of society—of its mediating institutions and its members—to attempt to answer that question both in theory and in practice. That attempt requires freedom even as it tries to advance freedom. But the freedom required and sought is always freedom tied to purpose.

Participants

Stephen Bates
Author
Cambridge, Massachusetts

Peter L. Berger
Institute for the Study of
Economic Culture
Boston University

Frithjof Bergmann
Department of Philosophy
University of Michigan

Francis Canavan, S.J.
Department of Political
Science
Fordham University

Dean C. Curry
Department of History and
Political Science
Messiah College

James Finn
Freedom House

Raymond Duncan Gastil
Coz Cob, Connecticut

Mary Ann Glendon
Harvard Law School

Martin Golding
School of Law
Duke University

Liah Greenfeld
Department of Sociology
Harvard University

Kent R. Hill
Institute on Religion and
Democracy

Richard G. Hutcheson, Jr.
Vienna, Virginia

Joachim Maitre
College of Communication
Boston University

Maria McFadden
The Human Life Review

Joshua Muravchik
American Enterprise Institute

Kenneth A. Myers
Powhatan, Virginia

Richard John Neuhaus
New York City

David Novak
Department of Religious
Studies
University of Virginia

James Nuechterlein
New York City

Stephen Post
Center for Biomedical Ethics
Case Western Reserve
University

Nina Shea
Puebla Institute

Paul T. Stallsworth
Creswell, North Carolina

Andrew Sullivan
Harvard University

Michael Warder
The Rockford Institute

George Weigel
Ethics and Public Policy
Center

Phyllis Zagano
College of Communication
Boston University